GOD 3:16

Ten Ways
God Shows His Love

T. K. Anderson

ENTRUSTED MINISTRIES
Connecting your Story with God's Story

Scottsdale, Arizona

Published by Entrusted Ministries
Scottsdale, Arizona (USA)

Acknowledgments:
Editing: Daniel Johnson
Interior Design: Karen Stuart
Cover Design: David Landis

©2023, T.K. Anderson God 3:16 - 10 Ways God Shows His Love

First edition: September 2023

Printed in the United States of America

To those who dare to dream,
Who find solace in the written Word,
And embark on journeys beyond the page,
This book is for you.

To the ones who believe in the power of God's love,
Who see the beauty in every story told,
And embrace the love that Jesus unveils,
This book is dedicated to you.

To the unwavering support of family and friends,
Whose love and encouragement fuel my passion,
And whose belief in me keeps me striving,
This book is a tribute to your unwavering presence.

To the late nights and early mornings,
To the struggles and triumphs,
To every joyous revelation and heart-wrenching revelation,
This book is a verse to the journey of creation.

May its pages awaken your soul, ignite your spirit,
And inspire you to paint your own stories,
A story ordained by God and anchored in His love.

With heartfelt gratitude and love,

T.K. Anderson

CONTENTS

Introduction vii

1. The God Who **Leads** You (Joshua 3:16) 13

2. The God Who **Defends** You (Daniel 3:16) 29

3. The God Who **Appoints** You (Mark 3:16) 47

4. The God Who **Loves** You (John 3:16) 67

5. The God Who **Heals** You (Acts 3:16) 85

6. The God Who **Indwells** You (1 Corinthians 3:16) 103

7. The God Who **Pardons** You (2 Corinthians 3:16) 123

8. The God Who **Calms** You (2 Thessalonians 3:16) 139

9. The God Who **Guides** You (2 Timothy 3:16) 157

10. The God Who **Challenges** You (Revelation 3:16) 173

Conclusion 191

Introduction

God loves numbers. In fact, there is an entire book describing how the children of Israel wandered in the wilderness for 40 years. You know what the book is called? The book of Numbers. In the Bible numbers are often used symbolically, and carry spiritual and metaphorical meaning, providing deeper insights and messages.

God, like a mathematician, is known for His precision, order, and the intricate design of the universe. Just as a mathematician creates elegant mathematical equations to describe the workings of the world, God, as the ultimate Creator, has established fundamental laws and principles that govern the universe. We also see this design in the layout of the Bible where numbers are very important.

For example…

One represents unity and uniqueness and is associated with God's oneness, sovereignty, and the concept of absolute truth. The number two symbolizes the idea of contrast and partnership. It can represent division, choice, or the need for witnesses. Three signifies completeness, divine perfection, and the Trinity. Seven symbolizes perfection, completeness, and divine order. It is a number often associated with God's work and the Sabbath day of rest. Ten signifies completeness in a divine order. It is associated with the Ten Commandments, representing the moral law. There are many more examples of the care and thought put into the Bible as it relates to the significance God puts on numbers and dates.

Introduction

Did you know, though, that God loves something far more than numbers. He loves people. God is not known as a mathematician although the universe operates on His foundational principles. He is a Creator, Father, and Redeemer. It is impossible to fully describe God. We can't get our minds around His infinite nature and what the Bible describes as His unsearchable ways. In fact, the Bible says God's ways are beyond finding out. However (and this is a big however), God has made known to us His nature, His will, and His plan for our lives. Most importantly, God wants us to know that He is the source of all love.

This book began as a sermon series delivered live. As you read these words, my intention is that the truth behind them will come alive to you. As you read, I invite you to a journey of discovering God and the ways He shows His love to us.

Donald Knuth, a retired computer science professor at Stanford, took five years to study every chapter 3 verse 16 in the Bible. He studied every 3:16 verse of each book of the Bible thinking his analysis was going to be random. What he found was that many of the great truths of the Bible and attributes of God were found in those verses. He describes the study as a turning point in his life.

The universe is infinite and gazing into the night sky is a profound, humbling, and even frightening experience as we contemplate the blackness of space. But amidst this expanse of the universe, amidst the beauty of creation, there exists a profound and indescribable force that pervades every corner of existence – that force is a person. Not a woman or a man, but a life-giving Spirit with personal qualities. God is not merely a distant deity, but an ever-present force of love and compassion. The search to understand the nature of God and to discover how He reveals His love has captivated the hearts and minds of humanity throughout the ages. In this book, "God 3:16: Ten Ways God Shows His Love," we embark on a journey of exploration and revelation, delving into ten awe-inspiring attributes of God as described in the sacred verses of chapter 3, verse 16, in the Bible.

Within the confines of these 3:16 Stories, a wellspring of God's insight awaits. It is through these ten attributes we catch glimpses of God's generous love and begin to fathom the depths of His grace. Each attribute unfolds like a delicate petal, revealing a unique facet of God's character, and inviting us to a deeper understanding of His immeasurable love for each of us. The question then becomes, are we ready to move forward with God?

Before we do, let's take a look at the significance of these God qualities we are about to explore. Someone wisely said that what you think of when you think of God is the most important thing about you. That is because your ideas of God, whether He exists, whether His promises are true and whether He is fair and worth following form the basis of your belief system. Even before all the rules you may try to follow and the morality you attempt to model, the God who underlies it all is the linchpin, the capstone to your worldview. And your worldview then informs your day-to-day actions. In other words, your beliefs acted upon become your life.

An attribute is a characteristic or quality associated with a person. It describes a particular aspect or feature of something. Attributes can be used to provide information, describe properties, or classify and distinguish objects or individuals. When discussing a person, attributes could include physical characteristics like height, hair color, or eye color, as well as personality traits such as kindness, intelligence, or creativity.

Attributes are essential for categorizing and understanding the characteristics and properties of objects, individuals, or concepts. They help provide a more comprehensive and detailed description of the subject under consideration.

So, when we talk about the attributes of God, we are drilling down to the very nature of God, His character and characteristics. Studying theology is important. Right doctrine informs right practice and is vital for a well-balanced spiritual life. But underneath it all is the fact that we can know God, that He is gracious, powerful, wise, merciful, all powerful, all knowing and holy.

The best news of all? God is accessible to us because He has revealed Himself to us in Jesus. You see, the 3:16 stories all lead back to Jesus. So our journey will take us throughout the Bible, it will introduce us to the most colorful set of characters, and it will fill our minds with beautiful truths expressed in particular Bible verses. But ultimately, all roads lead back to Jesus.

When it comes to the attributes of God, they are all found in the person of Jesus Christ. Are you ready to begin the adventure? The numbers three one six are the roadmap that centers around what matters each day. To live and move and have our being in Jesus and to live out loud that relationship one day at a time.

Introduction

Chapter 1

The God Who Leads You

Joshua 3:16

Attribute: God is Gracious

I have learned something important over the years: It is one thing to have an answer, but it is better to know the answer.

There was once a student who answered "accurately" on a pop quiz from his teacher. But he ran into a problem because he didn't answer "correctly." This student ended up receiving a 0% on his quiz.

Here are his answers to the teacher's questions:

- Where was the Declaration of Independence signed? *At the bottom of the page.*

- What is the main reason for divorce? *Marriage*

- What can you never eat for breakfast? *Lunch & dinner.*

- What looks like half an apple? *The other half.*

13

- How can a man go eight days without sleeping? *No problem, he sleeps at night.*

- How can you lift an elephant with one hand? *You will never find an elephant that has only one hand.*

- If you had three apples and four oranges in one hand and four apples and three oranges in the other hand, what would you have? *Very large hands*

- If it took eight men ten hours to build a wall, how long would it take four men to build it? *No time at all, the wall is already built.*

- How can you drop a raw egg onto a concrete floor without cracking it? *Any way you want, concrete floors are very hard to crack.*

- What is the main reason for failing a test? *Exams.*

In terms of our Christian experience, I've learned over the years that many individuals have a limited understanding of God's character and nature. How well would you do on a quiz about God's character and nature? Kind of scary, right?

It's possible that daily concerns and challenges, or a lack of discussion about God in your upbringing may contribute to your apprehension. It's important to note that simply having knowledge about God is not the same as discovering who He is.

I bring this up not to discourage you, but to encourage you to pursue a deeper understanding and relationship with God.

The book you are reading is based on a sermon series entitled, "Discovering God: Ten Ways God Shows His Love."

In preparing for it, I realized something fascinating. Embedded within the pages of the Bible, there are hidden gems about God's love offered in plain sight. Most people, even those without much Bible knowledge, have heard of John 3:16. But did you know there are at least nine more "3:16 verses" just like it?

There are a total of forty-nine "3:16 verses." Twenty-eight in the Old Testament and twenty-one in the New Testament. Yet within this great group of passages, there are ten that reveal the character and nature of God in a surprising way.

In this book we will unpack ten "3:16 verses" and discover how each one teaches us something different about God and reveals just how much He loves us.

We begin with learning about the God who leads us.

Let me ask, who's leading your life? Is it you? Is it someone else? Maybe it's a situation or some type of substance? Or perhaps something completely different. If it's not God, then you're experiencing way less than what God has for your life.

I want to share with you how God shows His love by leading us in three distinct ways.

To uncover these three ways let's explore Joshua 3:16: *"The water above that point began backing up a great distance away at a town called Adam, which is near Zarethan. And the water below that point flowed on to the Dead Sea until the riverbed was dry. Then all the people crossed over near the town of Jericho."*

The first thing we learn about God's leadership is....

15

GOD PREVENTS THINGS FROM OVERWHELMING YOU

When we find ourselves in difficult situations, our perspective can shift as we realize that the Lord has either placed us there or allowed it to happen for reasons that may currently be unknown to us.

This was the case for a couple named Russell and Darlene Deibler who arrived in New Guinea in 1938 on their first wedding anniversary to spread the word of Christ. However, when the Japanese invaded the East Indies, they were separated and both suffered greatly. Darlene was imprisoned in a military camp and faced forced labor, near starvation, and various illnesses. One day she was even singled out for execution.

As she was taken to a death camp and locked in a cell with the words, "This person must die," written on the door, Darlene found herself singing a song she learned as a child in Sunday school. She felt strong arms around her and realized that though her captors could lock her in, they could not lock out her Lord. She knew that she was in His will, and that God's will would never put her where His presence could not sustain her. This assurance helped her to endure impossible times and even saved her life.[1]

J.I. Packer, a well-known theologian and writer of the best-selling book *Knowing God*, once wrote, "He knows the way He taketh, even if for the moment we do not."

In the biblical story Joshua and the people of Israel are just outside of the land that was promised to them by God through Moses. The only problem was that Moses had just passed away and the river Jordan was at a flood stage. There was no way to ferry across, trod across, or walk across. They were in a hopeless situation and didn't know what to do.

Have you ever been there in life? On the edge of relief, chasing the coattails of success, or being a whisper away from the one thing needed for all to be well?

The people of God were in that exact spot until God showed up and showed them His love. The Bible tells us that, *"The water above that point began backing up a great distance away at a town called Adam, which is near Zarethan."* (Joshua 3:16a) What's going on here?

The first thing we know is the people of God were waiting at a place on the east side of the Jordan River just across from the city of Jericho. Joshua and the spiritual leaders at the time were given instructions from God to step into the river with the Ark of the Covenant, and at the command of God the Jordan River would dry up so they would be able to cross.

And that's exactly what happened as "The water...began backing up a great distance away."

Some have asked how something like this happens? It's a good question and I don't have enough time to go into all the details, but there are two possible solutions. One would be an absolute divine miracle that took place as God breaks the natural laws of the universe and commands the water to halt and that's it. It wouldn't be beyond God's capabilities since He spoke the entire universe into existence.

Another option could be that God utilized a natural barrier to stop the water upstream as the Bible describes. The idea is that an earthquake caused dirt cliffs upstream to collapse, temporarily blocking the river and allowing the Israelites to cross. This has happened in recorded history and even occurred at the same location mentioned in the Bible, in the city of Adam, 20 miles upstream of Jericho, in 1927. The landslide blocked the river for 21 hours. An expert in the field, Abba Niv, regional engineer at the Israeli Soil Conservation Service, has spoken about this theory, noting that it is not only logical but also possible. He personally witnessed a similar event north of the ancient city of Adam. A cliff about 100 feet high fell into the river and closed the streambed for several hours, and a herd of cattle was able to cross the river to feed on the other side. The water rose above the landslide and cut through the temporary dam within 24 hours, and everything returned to normal.[2]

It's worth noting that this theory is just that, a theory, but it can be encouraging for those new to the Bible to know that this miracle story has a scientific explanation plausible to someone knowledgeable in the field.

Simply put, God made the laws of physics, and He knows how to use them as He wants. So, whether God broke the laws of physics or used them as He wanted to, either way, the timing of the event constitutes a miracle.

What it means for you today is God shows His love for you by preventing the flood waters of your situation from overwhelming you. He stops it upstream. He causes the waters of your situation from overtaking you. In many ways He prevents it from reaching you because He's protecting you.

Psalm 91:4 tells us, *"He will shelter you with His wings. His faithful promises are your armor and protection."*

Psalm 18:30 says, *"God's way is perfect. All the LORD's promises prove true. He is a shield for all who look to him for protection."*

Isaiah 25:4-5 declares, *"But you are a tower of refuge to the poor, O LORD, a tower of refuge to the needy in distress. You are a refuge from the storm and a shelter from the heat. For the oppressive acts of ruthless people are like a storm beating against a wall, or like the relentless heat of the desert. But you silence the roar of foreign nations. As the shade of a cloud cools relentless heat, so the boastful songs of ruthless people are stilled."*

So the first thing we learn is that God leads us by preventing the challenges of life from overwhelming us. He protects us from many things heading our way.

The second thing we learn about God's leadership is…

GOD REMOVES THINGS IN FRONT OF YOU

What's the largest item ever moved? A natural gas drilling platform holds the record as the largest object ever moved by human beings. It is located off the coast of Norway and weighs an astounding 1.2 million tons and stands 1,548 feet tall. To transport it to its location 174 miles away from the Norwegian coast, 10 tugboats were used. The journey was slow with a speed of one knot per hour, taking a total of seven days and six hours to reach its destination. Once it arrived, the tugboats formed a star formation around the platform to support it as it was stabilized. Columns were driven 118 feet into the seabed to hold it in place.[3]

Like that 1.2-million-ton giant, you and I face giants of our own that need to be moved. But we lack the strength and resources to do it on our own. We need God's help.

In fact, for many of you, your giant is always nearby, vying for your attention and hoping to be the first voice you hear when you wake up. He wants to fill your thoughts with worries and stress, to make you dread the day before it even begins. If you find yourself feeling anxious before starting your day, it's a sign that your giant has been by your bedside.[4]

He doesn't stop there, he follows you throughout your day, always lurking close by, whispering in your ear and shadowing your steps. He checks your schedule, reads your mail, and constantly tells you that you're not good enough, that you come from a long line of losers, and that you've been dealt a bad hand.

He's like the Goliath of old, taunting, teasing, boasting, and echoing his claims from one hillside to the other. Remember how Goliath bragged? *"For forty days, twice a day, morning and evening, the Philistine giant strutted in front of the Israelite army."* (1 Samuel 17:16)

In the same way, your giant will try to dominate you with devastating challenges such as debt, disaster, disease, deceit, and depression. But remember that you can defeat your giant by focusing on God first.

Max Lucado writes, *"Focus on giants, you stumble. Focus on God, your giants tumble."*[5]

Let's discover the second way God leads us. The text says, *"the water below that point flowed on to the Dead Sea until the riverbed was dry."* (Joshua 3:16b)

What's going on here? As the water stopped 20 miles upstream, the current eventually pulled the remaining water south and into the Dead Sea. Gravity did its job and by doing so the riverbed became dry. Imagine the scene. As the spiritual leaders stepped into the raging river, the size of the water began to dissipate. The size of the river slowly decreased. From 500 yards wide to 100 yards wide to 20 yards wide. Eventually a dry riverbed was all that remained.

In terms of what it meant for the people of God, the obstacle, their giant, had been moved. All that stood in their way to inherit all God had for them was now gone. Imagine the freedom they felt. Imagine the joy they experienced. Imagine the hope that filled their hearts.

Throughout the pages of the Bible, God reveals how He is constantly removing barriers and defeating the giants in the lives of those who follow Him.

We see this in the story of David and Goliath. We see this in the story of Moses and the Red Sea. We see this in the story of Paul and Silas locked up in a Philippian Prison. In all three cases, God removes the obstacle standing in the way so the people of God can move forward.

God guided David's stone and removed Goliath. God split the Red Sea and removed the barricade. God unshackled the bonds and removed their constraint. And He can do it for you today.

Do you know why God loves to move the obstacles in your life? Because He cares for you. That's the motivation. He's moved by His love for you. Look at these three situations in the Bible when Jesus was moved by someone who was hurting and needed help.

One day a leper approached Jesus and asked Him if He was willing to help him. *"Will you remove this giant of sickness?", the leper asked. Moved with compassion, Jesus reached out and touched him. "I am willing," He said. "Be healed!"* (Mark 1:41)

Another time, when Mary the sister of Lazarus began weeping about the loss of her brother, the Bible describes in vivid detail what happened in Jesus' heart for one of His friends, *"When Jesus saw her weeping, and the Jews who had come with her also weeping, He was deeply moved in His spirit."* (John 11:33)

And a few moments later, as Jesus stood by the tomb of Lazarus we read, *"Then Jesus, deeply moved again, came to the tomb. It was a cave, and a stone lay against it."* (John 11:38)

And within the next few minutes, the giant of death was moved as Jesus commanded the body of Lazarus to come out of that grave. His words moved a dead man to life again. Here's how the Bible captures this miraculous moment.

[43]"When (Jesus) had said these things, He cried out with a loud voice, 'Lazarus, come out.' [44]The man who had died came out, his hands and feet bound with linen strips, and his face wrapped with a cloth. Jesus said to them, 'Unbind him, and let him go.'" (John 11:43-44)

In all these examples we discover that God leads His people

because He's moved with compassion for them. Please understand that the miracles of God are not done to impress unbelievers or provide God an opportunity to flex His spiritual muscle. When God removes barriers in our life it's rooted in His concern for us.

This provides a great picture for us in our search to learn more about the God who leads us.

We've learned so far that God leads you by preventing challenges from overwhelming you and by removing those in front of you.

The final thing we learn about God's leadership is…

GOD PROVIDES THE WAY FORWARD FOR YOU

One day, Georgene Johnson, a 42-year-old woman, ran a marathon by accident in downtown Cleveland. She had accidentally lined up with the wrong group at the starting line, not the 10K group she had intended to participate in, but the full 26-mile marathon group. It wasn't until 4 miles into the race that she realized her mistake, but instead of quitting, she kept going and finished the race in 4 hours and 4 minutes. What she said afterward is remarkable, "This isn't the race I trained for. This isn't the race I entered. But, for better or worse, this is the race I'm in."

The story concludes with a powerful sentence, *"Then all the people crossed over near the town of Jericho."* (Joshua 3:16c)

With the giant in front of them removed and the water upstream being prohibited from overwhelming them, the people of God now had an opportunity to move forward into all that God had in store for their life. The promised land awaited them.

In his book *Wild Goose Chase*, Mark Batterson writes, "When Christianity turns into a noun, it becomes a turnoff. Christianity was always intended to be a verb. And more specifically, an action verb. The title of the book of Acts says it all, doesn't it? It's not the book of Ideas or Theories or Words. It's the book of Acts. If the twenty-first-century church said less and did more, maybe we would have the same kind of impact the first-century church did."[6]

Batterson is on to something. How many times has God cleared away the obstacles in your life and you refused, delayed, or dismissed the opportunity in front of you?

One of the ways God shows His love for you is to provide a way forward into new opportunities and new ministries. When we delay or deny those new openings, we become like the people of God in this story if they had refused to cross over the now-dry riverbed.

Let me encourage you to not stay on the current side of your issue, it's time to cross over. It's time to move forward. It's time to put the past behind you and move into the new land God has promised you.

During one of Jesus' last teaching moments before He went to the cross, He taught His followers the importance of moving forward with opportunities provided them by God. We find this story in Matthew chapter twenty-five. It's called the parable of the talents. In the story three workers each receive a certain portion of money. One guy buries his money doing nothing with it, while the other two workers double the money entrusted to them. When the owner returns the workers present their results. The two workers who doubled their dollars are told, *"Well done, good and faithful servant. You have been faithful over a little I will set you over much."* (Matthew 25:23) While the lazy worker is basically fired on the spot!

Batterson's comments on this are striking, "Some of us live as if we expect to hear God say, "Well thought, good and faithful servant!" or "Well said, good and faithful servant!" God isn't going to say either of those things. There is only one commendation, and it is the by-product of pursuing God-ordained passions: "Well done, good and faithful servant!"

What door has God opened for you that you have yet to walk through? What obstacle has been removed but you're stagnantly standing as if it's still there? What riverbed has been removed of all its water, yet you are refusing to cross over?

I need to pray about it some more, you might say. It may be true in some cases, but if the way has been made clear, the time to pray about it is done, and the time to move is now upon you!

Prayer is not always necessary for certain actions. Loving your neighbor, giving generously, and serving sacrificially are actions God has already made clear through His teachings. Instead of praying about these actions, it's important to take action.

Instead of praying about:

- Filling out an application, just fill it out.

- Making a call, just make the call.

- Packing a truck, just pack it.

- Writing a check, just write it.

- Setting an appointment, just set it.

- Having a conversation, just have it.

- Making a move, just make it.

In other words, stop talking about doing something for God and just do it.[7]

CONCLUSION

In this chapter, we have seen that God leads you in three specific ways:

1. He Prevents things from overwhelming you.
2. He Removes things in front of you.
3. He Provides the way forward for you.

In all three of these areas, we have come to understand that God does this because of His great care and compassion for you. Simply put, God loves you and shows you His love by leading you through the challenges, struggles, and battles in life.

The attribute of God we learn from this is God's grace. God's grace is part of His divine nature. It's baked into who He is. A graceful God is a God who wants to lead His creation into a place of safety. A place of purpose. A place of flourishing and success.

God's grace is what allows us to defeat the giants in our life.

God's grace is what propels us into the new opportunities that await us. God's grace is what protects us from the water upstream looking for a way to drown out the plan and purpose of God in our life. God's grace is what propels Him to remove obstacles and open the pathway to God's best in our life.

As a final thought, there's another element to God's grace you may need today.

In a small prison cell in Detroit, Robert Garth, a former track star and confessed murderer, was at peace. The detectives investigating his case were in shock and confusion as they verified his story and went over old files. Robert's story was true, every detail checked out. But one thing puzzled the detectives, why would a murderer who had committed the perfect crime come forward and implicate himself 15 years later? He had gotten away with it, no one knew.

However, there was one person who knew, the person who mattered most, himself. Now that he had confessed, he was free from the burden of his guilt. He was able to focus on the book someone had given him, a Bible. The section that drew him in was the book of Psalms. It was as if someone had recorded his thoughts over the years, an x-ray of his soul. Robert read about a God of grace who could shoulder the heaviest, deadliest burden and found the promise of true forgiveness.

The trial judge, seeing Robert's remorse, was lenient. He had voluntarily confessed and accepted the consequences. The sentence was short for a murder case.

Robert would later say, "My time in prison was easy compared to the fifteen years I lived with that crime in my mind….Nothing they could ever do to me, even incarcerating me for the rest of my life, could measure up to the imprisonment of my own guilt during the fifteen years of hiding my sin."[8]

Guilt is a giant of terrible weight. But Robert finally brought down that giant with forgiveness found in Jesus Christ.[9]

Maybe you're reading this and you've never given your life over to Jesus Christ. The burden of your sin weighs heavy on your heart, and you feel as though you're in a prison of guilt or shame. Listen, you don't have to stay there. God is ready to lead you out. Surrender your life to Christ today and come to the cross for forgiveness like millions upon millions of others have done before you.

At the cross, you'll find freedom. At the cross you'll find forgiveness. At the cross you'll find God's amazing grace. Don't wait another day. Today is the day you find freedom and forgiveness for your soul.

Chapter 2

The God Who Defends You

Daniel 3:16

Attribute: God is All-Powerful

If you were accused of a crime you didn't commit, how would you respond? Would you defend yourself? Would you put up a fight? Perhaps you would state your case forcefully and repeatedly so everyone would know you were not guilty.

If you reacted in this way, you wouldn't be out of the ordinary. Most of us would agree we have a right to and in many cases need to defend ourselves against false accusations.

It's part of our Americanized DNA. And built into the Constitution is the idea of being "Innocent until proven guilty."

But what if you were guilty? How would you respond? Would you fight for your innocence with the same fervency, or would

29

you admit your guilt in the hopes of getting an easier penalty? Would it depend on how much evidence the prosecution has?

These types of decisions are being played out every day in courtrooms across our country and around the world. In a similar way, this type of controversial court battle is being played out in our next "3:16 Story."

Let's see what it says: Shadrach, Meshach, and Abednego replied, "*Oh Nebuchadnezzar, we do not need to defend ourselves before you.*" (Daniel 3:16)

In the last chapter we discussed that most of us know John 3:16 in the Bible, but what we also learned is that there are nine more "3:16 verses" just like it. And each "3:16 verse" tells us a little bit more about who God is and just how much He loves us.

In this text, we bump into three Hebrew heroes who refuse to cave in to the cultural norms of their society. Although the events of their story happened over 2,500 years ago, the way they handled their situation will impact your life today.

The main message of our heroes is to never cave in to the cultural pressures surrounding you because you have an all-powerful God behind you. When you stand up, stand out, and stand strong for the Kingdom of God is precisely when your Christian life becomes breathtaking.

Kyle Idleman, author of *Not a Fan* writes, "I really hope you weren't looking for a book about Jesus the T-Ball coach, who will pat you on the head at the end of each game and tell you not to forget your free snow cone before you go home. When Jesus described the life of a follower, He described a risky adventure.

He is countercultural in an uncool way. And He loves you so much that He tells you the truth even when it is hard to hear. It's because He loves you that He talks more about repentance than forgiveness, more about surrender than salvation, more about sacrifice than happiness, and more about death than life. Following Jesus is anything but easy."[10]

We learn from Kyle that following Jesus is an exciting venture. It's a road less traveled, but it's a road we don't walk alone. So, let's discover how to be fully engaged followers of Jesus as we look at a compelling and captivating story found in chapter three of the book of Daniel.

Let's begin our story by first looking at...

THE SELF-IMPORTANCE OF A KING

The ancient world, like our world, was full of turmoil, intrigue, and cruelty. The Bible doesn't shy away from telling the truth about the limitations, frailty, and faults of our human condition. Yet what the Bible also provides is a way not only to survive through the chaos of this world but to thrive in the middle of it.

In John 17, Jesus reminds us to *"be in the world, but not of it."* Another time, In Matthew 5, Jesus told His disciples to be "salt and light" in the world. Salt is good for preserving things and light is good for making things visible. This means we are to have a formidable impact on our culture even though tyranny and pettiness happen all around us.

In Daniel chapter three, we are introduced to an insecure and arrogant king by the name of Nebuchadnezzar. He was a king of great status in the ancient world. At one time his kingdom (the kingdom of Babylon) ruled much of the known world. He had the fiercest warriors and the best cutting-edge technology in military warfare. Historians tell us the Babylonians made great contributions to the fields of mathematics, literature, and philosophy. They were a formidable empire.

Yet on the opposite side of those great contributions was a tyrannical rule that existed to crush and eradicate those who were not loyal to the throne. Worship to anything but the king would not be tolerated. In verse one we read, *"King Nebuchadnezzar made a gold statue ninety feet tall and nine feet wide and set it up on the plain of Dura in the province of Babylon."* (Daniel 3:1)

The purpose of this golden image was to proclaim to the world that the reign of Nebuchadnezzar would be forever. But like all tyrants, his days were numbered. Eventually the Babylonians would be overthrown and conquered by a rival nation. But not before God utilized the arrogance of the authoritarian king to reveal to the world something amazing about God's nature.

In Daniel chapter three, the Bible says the king sent messengers throughout his entire kingdom to gather all his leaders to the plain of Dura (modern-day Iraq). When the horns, pipes, and other instruments sounded, everyone was to bow down before the golden statue in an act of worship to Nebuchadnezzar. Here's how the Bible explains it, *"⁵When you hear the sound of the musical instruments, bow to the ground to worship King Nebuchadnezzar's gold statue. ⁶Anyone who refuses to obey will immediately be thrown into a blazing furnace."* (Daniel 3:5-6)

The king left no room for dissension, no room for tolerance, no room for opposing views. Bow or burn was the decree. What would you do in this situation? Would you be tempted to bow, or would the iron rod of your will steady your nerves as you stood against your culture in a divine act of holy insurrection and worship to God?

Regrettably, some of you are facing a situation like this today. The decree has been spoken. The trap has been set. The cultural norms have been dictated and if you refuse to bow, if you refuse to go along with the crowd, you'll be thrown into the furnace of social or career termination. Everything you've worked for will be burned at the altar of capitulation laying at the feet of cultural compromise.

In verse seven we find that *"all the people...bowed to the ground and worshiped the gold statue that King Nebuchadnezzar had set up."* (Daniel 3:7)

However, according to the text, there were three Hebrew leaders who decided to refuse the command of the king and in their moment of decision, their commitment to a heavenly King far outweighed the threat of an earthly king.

We capture their actions in verse 12, *"But there are some Jews—Shadrach, Meshach, and Abednego—whom you have put in charge of the province of Babylon. They pay no attention to you, Your Majesty. They refuse to serve your gods and do not worship the gold statue you have set up."* (Daniel 3:12)

In case you're not familiar with the historical context here, a few years prior to this event the people of Israel, God's people, were taken captive by king Nebuchadnezzar and carted off to

Babylon. A small remnant remained in Israel, but most of the people were taken captive, especially the young leaders with potential. Three of these young men were Shadrach, Meshach, and Abednego.

The ramifications of the king were swift. We read, *"[13]Then Nebuchadnezzar flew into a rage and ordered that Shadrach, Meshach, and Abednego be brought before him. When they were brought in,[14]Nebuchadnezzar said to them, 'Is it true, Shadrach, Meshach, and Abednego, that you refuse to serve my gods or to worship the gold statue I have set up? [15]I will give you one more chance to bow down and worship the statue I have made when you hear the sound of the musical instruments. But if you refuse, you will be thrown immediately into the blazing furnace. And then what god will be able to rescue you from my power?'"* (Daniel 3:13-15)

The first scene of our story captures the great struggle before us. Do we cave in, or do we stand courageous? Is God's power able to rescue us from the power of another? "What god will be able to rescue you from my power?" Nebuchadnezzar asked.

Winston Churchill once said, "To every man there comes in his lifetime that special moment when he is figuratively tapped on the shoulder and offered that chance to do a special thing, unique to him and fitted to his talents."[11]

The tap on the shoulder must have felt like a divine punch in the arm to these three young men. But either way, in their moment of truth, they responded in a way that still inspires the hearts and minds of believers today.

Let's continue our story by looking at...

THE STEADFASTNESS OF THEIR FAITH

Immediately following the king's threat of being roasted alive, our three heroes responded without reservation, *"¹⁶Shadrach, Meshach, and Abednego replied, 'Oh Nebuchadnezzar, we do not need to defend ourselves before you. ¹⁷If we are thrown into the blazing furnace, the God whom we serve is able to save us. He will rescue us from your power, Your Majesty. '"* (Daniel 3:16-17)

I love the determination of these young men. They were straightforward and unashamed. With ice water running through their veins, they answered the king's question of, what god will be able to rescue you, with an unwavering reply, "Ours, that's who!" The biblical reply was, "The God whom we serve is able to save us." But the bravado in their voice would have been unescapable.

Were they crazy? Did they lose their minds? Why in the world would they risk their lives like this? Or maybe they knew something. Maybe they understood something. Something at the core of their being.

- Something bigger than any king.

- Something deeper than any threat.

- Something more powerful than any furnace, no matter how hot it gets.

- Something that transcends a situation and provides deliverance no matter the outcome.

That's what they knew! And that's how they could say these powerful and life-altering words: "We do not need to defend ourselves before you."

These are the same words Peter used, *"Do you think God wants us to obey you or to obey him?"* (Acts 4:19 CEV)

These are the same words Paul used, *"These little troubles are getting us ready for an eternal glory that will make all our troubles seem like nothing."* (2 Cor. 4:17 CEV)

These are the same words Job used, *"But I know there is someone in heaven who will come at last to my defense."* (Job 19:25 GNT)

These are the same words Jesus used, *"Father, forgive them, for they don't know what they are doing."* (Luke 23:34)

In all five of these situations the response is the same. It's an understanding that something greater is happening in and through my situation. The situation is not here to define me, it is here to design me.

God, what are you wanting to do through me in this situation, that's the question! It's not, "Why me, God?" It's, "What are you doing through me, God?"

When we get to the place where our spiritual maturity is an automatic "What Now?" instead of a "Why Me?" that's when we will begin to have the bravery, steadfastness, and strength of these heroes of faith.

And just to make their point explicitly clear, they even went so far as to declare, *"But even if He doesn't, we want to make it clear to you, Your Majesty, that we will never serve your gods or worship the gold statue you have set up."* (Daniel 3:18)

Those are fightin' words for Nebuchadnezzar! He was mad at this point. Fuming, as if smoke was coming out of his ears. Think I'm exaggerating? Look at how the Bible describes the king at this point, *"Nebuchadnezzar was so furious with Shadrach, Meshach, and Abednego that his face became distorted with rage. He commanded that the furnace be heated seven times hotter than usual."* (Daniel 3:19)

His face was distorted with rage, did you catch that part? That's pretty mad! Imagine a D-1 narcissist not getting what he wants. That's the picture here. This king was so full of himself that there was no room for anyone's opinion but his own. In keeping with the king's command, the furnace was turned up seven times hotter and the suspense became even greater. What would happen? How would this all play out? Would God deliver them, or would they be burned alive?

Evangelist Billy Graham once asked the question, "What will you be like as a Christian ten years from now?" He continued, "Many will be walking with Christ and serving Him, but for others, there will be a tragedy because ten years from now they will have lost their burning zeal and love for Christ."[12]

For some, the firestorms of life can cause the burning zeal for Christ to go out. As the heat of our situation increases the desire for more of God can diminish. The cause for this is rooted in fear. We're afraid God won't come through or we're afraid the fire is too hot. We're afraid God has more important things to do than to be concerned about our life and situation. Listen, friend, don't be afraid. Don't fear, God has you covered.

In answering Graham's question, what kind of Christian you

will be in ten years will greatly depend on how you handle the fiery furnaces of your life between now and then.

Getting back to our story, in verses 20-23, the king had our three heroes bound and thrown into the furnace. In the process because the furnace was so hot, the king's soldiers died instantly as they threw Shadrach, Meshach, and Abednego into the fire.

What happens next is nothing short of a miracle, or better put, nothing short of a manifestation. The entire royal entourage was shocked to see with their own eyes what God did.

Let's continue our story by looking at...

THE SURPRISING RESULT

[24] *"But suddenly, Nebuchadnezzar jumped up in amazement and exclaimed to his advisers, 'Didn't we tie up three men and throw them into the furnace?' 'Yes, Your Majesty, we certainly did,' they replied.* [25] *'Look!' Nebuchadnezzar shouted. 'I see four men, unbound, walking around in the fire unharmed! And the fourth looks like a god!'*

"[26]Then Nebuchadnezzar came as close as he could to the door of the flaming furnace and shouted: 'Shadrach, Meshach, and Abednego, servants of the Most High God, come out! Come here!'" (Daniel 3:24-26)

This is where the enormous lesson of the story is brought home:

- In the midst of the fire, God was with them

- In the midst of the struggle, God was right there

- In the midst of the brawl, God was in the ring

- Their co-workers turned on them

- The culture caved in on them

- The king attempted to crush them

- But God showed up and was right there beside them

Isaiah 43:2 reminds us, *"When you go through deep waters, I will be with you. When you go through rivers of difficulty, you will not drown. When you walk through the fire of oppression, you will not be burned up; the flames will not consume you."*

Psalm 34:7 says, *"If you honor the LORD, his angel will protect you."* (CEV)

Are you starting to see why they had no need to defend themselves to the king? They knew God would be there and would deliver them if needed. You and I don't need to waste our precious time on this planet defending something God has already conquered. The battle was won and fought 2,000 years ago on a hill called Calvary.

When Christ died upon an old rugged cross and rose again from a cold, dark tomb three days later, all the enemies of God were defeated. At that moment every battle you and I will fight has already been won. We don't need to defend ourselves because He has already taken up our defense.

Some of you need to hear this today. You're in a battle. You're in a war. It feels as though the enemy has targeted your family and you're scared. It feels as though your enemies have turned up the furnace seven times hotter and you're bound up and being pushed to the edge. As your feet shuffle along the floor to slow down the inevitable, you can feel the heat of persecution growing. The heat of an unfair or unjust situation rises higher. The kings of the world seem to be dictating the rules and you wonder, where is God in all of this?

According to our "3:16 story", God's in the midst of the fire, awaiting your arrival.

- Let them throw you in, God's waiting.
- Let them think they've won, God's waiting.
- Let them hoot, holler, and shout for glee, God's waiting.
- You see friend, there isn't a body of water too deep that God cannot get to you.
- There isn't a river so fast that God cannot navigate the current.
- There isn't a fire so hot that God Himself cannot consume it.

And all of this is accomplished at the sheer sound of His voice. And determined at the pleasure of His will. God is sovereign over all.

In reading this "3:16 story" today, some might ask, who was the fourth man in the furnace? Many theologians believe the fourth man is evidence of something called a "Christophany," meaning an actual appearance of Jesus prior to His coming to us at Bethlehem. The theological term is a pre-incarnate appearance of Christ. Numerous times in the Old Testament God decided to make Himself known through various manifestations and today's story is one of those times.

Yet what happened next in the story is nothing short of amazing. Shadrach, Meshach, and Abednego came out of the fire and had no damage to their body, clothes, or hair. It was as if they never entered the fire at all. The Bible points out, *"Not a hair on their heads was singed, and their clothing was not scorched. They didn't even smell of smoke!"* (Daniel 3:27)

The king responded in complete amazement. His eyes did not deceive him. Therefore, he concluded, *"They defied the king's command and were willing to die rather than serve or worship any god except their own God. ²⁹Therefore, I make this decree: If any people, whatever their race or nation or language, speak a word against the God of Shadrach, Meshach, and Abednego, they will be torn limb from limb, and their houses will be turned into heaps of rubble. There is no other god who can rescue like this!"* (Daniel 3:28-29)

And just to put a cherry on top of this whole story, the king decided that all three of our Hebrew heroes would be promoted. Verse 30 tells us, *"Then the king promoted Shadrach, Meshach, and Abednego to even higher positions in the province of Babylon."* (Daniel 3:30)

Let's come full circle. We started out with a perplexing situation in which there seemed to be no end but destruction for our heroes. Yet, in the end the arrogant king promoted the faithful. Their need to defend their actions was completely unnecessary because God was the one prepared to defend them. They knew that truth. Do you know that truth as well?

No matter what you're facing today, as you put your complete trust in Jesus and quit trying to solve your situation on your own, He will give you the way out. As you spend time with Jesus, sometimes in the very fire of a furnace, His presence will be with you and as you honor God in your life, He will defend you, He will lead you, He will guide you, and He will promote you.

In some cases, you'll experience the promotion this side of Heaven like our three heroes of faith did. And other times, you will experience the promotion of God when you get to Heaven. Either way God is the one in charge and He decides the affairs of mankind. Our job, our challenge, our struggle, is to simply trust in Him and leave our defense in His hands.

CONCLUSION

Let me conclude with this...

In keeping with our theme, we are learning one new attribute of God in each one of our "3:16 Stories." The attribute or character trait we learn about God in Daniel 3:16 is the All-Powerful nature of God. The theological word for this is Omnipotent. Omni = "All" and Potent = "Powerful."

Omnipotent means to have unlimited power.

In his devotional *Forward*, Ron Moore puts it like this: "God's attribute of omnipotence means that God is able to do all that He desires to do. When He plans something, it will come to be. If He purposes something, it will happen. Nothing can prevent His plan. He has all the power to do whatever He decides to do."

Do you recall the king's question, what god will be able to

rescue you from my power? The answer to that is simple...our God! The king's question is like a 9-volt battery asking a nuclear power plant who has more power. It's a ridiculous comparison. God has more power at His command than the sum total of every sun in the entire universe, times a million! The situations we face stand up to that kind of power like a 9-volt battery.

- Scripture is clear that God is strong and mighty. (Psalm 24:8)

- Nothing is too hard for Him to accomplish. (Gen 18:14; Jer 32:17, 27; Luke 1:37)

- God is called "Almighty," He holds all power and authority. (2 Cor 6:18; Rev 1:8)

- He is "able to do immeasurably more than all we ask or imagine." (Eph 3:20)

Pastor and author John MacArthur provides a great insight for us: "Although such power might seem frightful, remember that God is good. He can do anything according to His infinite ability but will do only those things that are consistent with Himself."

God's infinite power is always in connection with His other traits such as His goodness, mercy, and grace. That's why we can trust Him and that's why His power is our best defense.

As a pastor I would be derelict in my duties if I didn't speak to you about one more thing regarding our need for God to defend us. The truth is that apart from the situation, struggles, and battles that we face in this life, there is a greater matter in which all of us will need Jesus to be our defense.

On April 23, 2021, on the website called Turn Back to God,

truck driver Matthew Page shared his story of what it means to have Jesus as His defender. Here's what he wrote: "About 15 years ago, I heard a story about Jesus being my attorney. I was driving down the road in the middle of the night in my 18-wheeler, I was all alone and was beside myself wondering and hoping that God would hear my prayers. And then, across my radio, a static-filled station told this beautiful story of a man who dreamed he went to Heaven after he died. Here's what he said…"[13]

After my time on earth came to an end. The first thing I remember is sitting on a bench in the waiting room of what I thought to be a courthouse. The doors opened and I was instructed to come in and have a seat by the defense table.

As I looked around, I saw the "prosecutor." He was a villainous-looking gent who snarled as he stared at me. He was the vilest person I have ever seen. I sat down and looked to my left and there sat my lawyer, a kind and gentle-looking man whose appearance seemed very familiar to me. The corner door flew open and there appeared the judge in full-flowing robes. He commanded an awesome presence as he moved across the room, and I couldn't take my eyes off him. As He took His seat behind the bench, He said "Let us begin."

The prosecutor rose and said, "My name is Satan, and I am here to show you why this man belongs in hell." He proceeded to tell of lies that I told, things that I stole, and in the past when I cheated others. Satan told of other horrible perversions that were once in my life, and the more he spoke the further down in my seat I sank. I was so embarrassed that I couldn't look at anyone, even my own lawyer, as the Devil told of sins that even I had completely forgotten about.

As upset as I was at Satan for telling all these things about me, I was equally upset at my representative who sat there silently not offering any form of defense at all. I know I had been guilty of those things, but I had done some good in my life — couldn't that at least equal out part of the harm I've done? Satan finished with a fury and said, "This man belongs in Hell. He is guilty of all that I have charged and there is not a person who can prove otherwise. Justice will finally be served this day."

When it was His turn, my lawyer first asked if He might approach the bench. The judge allowed this over the strong objection of Satan and beckoned Him to come forward. As He got up and started walking, I was able to see Him now in His full splendor and majesty. Now I realized why He seemed so familiar. It was Jesus representing me, my Lord and my Savior. He stopped at the bench and softly said to the judge, "Hi Dad," and then He turned to address the court.

"Satan was correct in saying that this man had sinned. I won't deny any of these allegations. And yes, the wages of sins is death, and this man deserves to be punished."

Jesus took a deep breath and turned to His Father with outstretched arms and proclaimed, "However, I died on the cross so that this person might have eternal life, and he has accepted Me as his Savior, so he is mine." My Lord continued with "his name is written in the book of life, and no one can snatch him from Me. Satan still does not understand yet, this man is not to be given justice, but rather mercy."

As Jesus sat down, He quietly paused, looked at His Father,

and replied, "There is nothing else that needs to be done, I've done it all."

The Judge lifted His mighty hand and slammed the gavel down, and the following words bellowed from His lips — "This man is free — the penalty for him has already been paid in full, case dismissed."

As my Lord led me away, I could hear Satan ranting and raving, "I won't give up, I'll win the next one." I asked Jesus as He gave me my instructions on where to go next, "Have you ever lost a case?"

Christ lovingly smiled and said, "Everyone that has come to me and asked Me to represent them has received the same verdict as you, Paid in Full."

Have you asked Jesus to be your defender…both in this life and the next? If you haven't you can do that today.

Chapter 3

The God Who Appoints You

Mark 3:16

Attribute: God is Wise

Hal Donaldson grew up near San Francisco, California as the son of a pastor. When he was 12 years old, his parents were hit by a drunk driver. His father died, and his mother was seriously injured. To make ends meet, they went on welfare. "I experienced the shame of poverty," Donaldson says. "I had holes in my shoes and clothes. When you're teased in school for being poor or walking into supermarkets with food stamps, you feel less than others. And you just try to escape that."

He managed to do just that. Donaldson went to college, earned a degree, and turned his focus to making money for himself. "I went through a period where I was self-centered," he said. "I was just trying to claw my way out of insignificance. The problem is, in trying to escape that life, it's easy to neglect others along the way. I was the guy that would see a homeless person and cross the street. My focus was on climbing to the top instead of helping those trying to climb with me."

In 1990, Hal was 23 years old, fresh out of college, and found himself in Calcutta, India. He was writing a book about feeding hungry children. He ended up meeting and interviewing Mother Teresa. "She was so humble," Donaldson says.

After their interview, Mother Teresa had a question for him: "Young man, what are you doing to help the poor?" He told her the truth. He was young and had just gotten his degree in journalism. He wasn't focused on helping others. With a smile on her face, Mother Teresa said, "Everyone can do something." Those words struck a deep chord in the heart of Hal Donaldson.[14]

They are the words that changed the trajectory of Hal's life. According to Forbes magazine, Hal and his team now operate one of the top 50 charities in the United States.[15]

How did Hal get from Calcutta to Forbes over the past 33 years? You'll have to wait until the end of the chapter for the conclusion of his story. But for now, I can say Hal finally came to a place in his life where he understood God had appointed him to something big. Something larger and bigger than anything he could have imagined. Something, in part, driven by the deep loss he experienced at 12 years of age. It was an appointment to share the love of Christ with those experiencing loss.

Is it true that God appoints you and I do to His will? According to our next "3:16 Story," the answer is yes. Let's take a look.

"And (Jesus) appointed the Twelve; and to Simon He added

the name Peter" (Mark 3:16 BLB).

This Bible verse is the beginning of a short listing of the original Twelve Apostles of Jesus. Following verse sixteen we find eleven more names of the young men who were called by Jesus to establish the foundations of His ministry through the Church. They were appointed by Him to carry out His work.

Does God still appoint (choose/call/pick) people to do His work or did this stop after the original Twelve?

In his letter to the believers in Thessalonica, Paul reminds them God had chosen them to hear and receive the gospel. *"My dear friends, God loves you, and we know He has chosen you to be His people."* (1 Thessalonians 1:4 CEV) They were called to give the life-changing message of grace away, as well as hearing and receiving it. *"We begged, encouraged, and urged each of you to live in a way that would honor God. He is the one who chose you to share in His own kingdom and glory."* (1 Thessalonians 2:12 CEV)

In a similar letter to new believers in Rome, Paul emphasizes five times in the opening seven verses this idea of being called or set apart for God's purpose. *"I am writing to all of you in Rome who are loved by God and are called to be His own holy people."* (Romans 1:7) He continues in verse eight to show enthusiasm about the news that their "faith is proclaimed in all the world." (Romans 1:8)

In his letter to the Corinthians, Paul once again takes a moment to teach these new Christians that God specifically chooses each of us for specific roles. *"First, God chose some people to be apostles and prophets and teachers for the church. But, He also chose some to work miracles or heal the sick or help others or be leaders or speak different kinds of languages."* (1 Corinthians 1:28 CEV)

In each of these passages it's clear God is the one appointing, and it is we who are pursuing that appointment.

Every four years we elect a new president in the United States and one of the tasks of our new leader is to appoint representatives to other countries around the world on our behalf. The President gets to appoint the head of State and other very important departments. I've always wondered what it would be like to be appointed to something important like that.

But did you know that according to the Bible, you and I are appointed to something far better and far bigger than a governmental office? We've been appointed by God to represent Him to the world.

Today, I'd like to share three things about God and the way He appoints us.

Let's begin by first understanding…

WHEN GOD RETAINS YOU

Retaining talent at the top level can be costly. Whether it's the world of high finance or chasing championship titles in sports, winning will cost you. According to U.S. News and World Report, Wells Fargo's top executive made $24 million in 2022. While JPMorgan Chase reported it paid its chief executive $34 million.[16]

If those yearly earnings seem crazy, they are dwarfed in

comparison to the top talent in sports. The top three players in sports are Lionel Messi, Cristiano Ronaldo, and Patrick Mahomes; with combined contracts in excess of $1.7 billion in multi-year deals.[17] Messi and Ronaldo are famous for their athletic talent on the soccer field, while Mahomes was Super Bowl bound again as one of the top Quarterbacks in the NFL. These examples show us that retention is not cheap.

However, when it comes to your spiritual life God spared no expense in His quest to retain you to be a member of His team. That's how I want you to begin thinking about this. You and I would be overjoyed if someone in business, sports, or another endeavor offered us a multi-year multi-million-dollar contract. But do we get equally excited about the reality of Christ paying the ultimate price for our spiritual freedom?

The price Jesus paid to secure our redemption far exceeds any financial cost this world could come up with. Twice in back-to-back chapters, Paul reminds us, *"You were bought with a price. So glorify God in your body."* (1 Corinthians 6:20) *"God paid a high price for you, so don't be enslaved by the world."* (1 Corinthians 7:23)

All of this is a reminder we have been redeemed by Christ and that our redemption was paid for at the cross which leads us to an appointment with God. Or better yet, an appointment from God.

What has God appointed you to do? According to the Bible, there are three ways God appoints you when you become a follower of Jesus.

The first is with your Connection with God as an individual. Our "3:16 Story" tells us, *"And (Jesus) appointed the Twelve; and to Simon He added the name Peter."* (Mark 3:16 BLB) The first part of this story reminds us that with God, everything is about the individual. God doesn't look at you as a number or random person. As our world grows increasingly cold and digital, it's the reverse of God's design for us. He looks at everyone as a special part of His creation. Every person matters. Every person counts. Every individual is important to God. Don't isolate yourself from God. Step into all that God has for your life. Embrace your future today by first connecting with God on an individual level.

When God calls you, He calls you by name. He calls you for a purpose. *"Do not fear, for I have redeemed you; I have called you by your name; you are Mine!"* (Isaiah 43:1 BSB)

The world wants to isolate you and keep you in fear. God wants to include you in His kingdom and invite you to enjoy His family. Don't ever think your life doesn't matter, because you matter to God.

- You may be lonely today.

- You may feel isolated today.

- You may live in fear or anxiety today.

In all these places, know and understand that God can lead you out. He leads you when you come to realize that God appoints you to be in a personal, individual, and specific relationship with Him. As you walk in that each day, those other worries melt away.

The second way God appoints you as a follower of Jesus is to reach your family. As we look back to our "3:16 verse" we find a man named Simon in the center of the discussion. *"And (Jesus) appointed the Twelve; and to Simon He added the name Peter."*

(Mark 3:16 BLB) In order to see the entirety of the story I need to take you back a few chapters.

During the initial gathering phase of His first followers, Jesus identified two sets of brothers. In Mark one we read, *"16Passing alongside the Sea of Galilee, (Jesus) saw Simon and Andrew the brother of Simon casting a net into the sea...19And going on a little farther, He saw James the son of Zebedee and John his brother, who were in their boat mending the nets."* (Mark 1:16-19)

In both cases Jesus brought an individual along with a family member. We see this throughout the life and ministry of Jesus. In many ways we have this backward today. We tend to individualize our experience with God so much that when we hit a bumpy road in sharing our faith with our family, we immediately close up shop and cease our efforts. But that's a mistake. We shouldn't close up shop, we simply need to change our strategy.

If you have unbelieving family members, remember the Bible tells us, *"Not even His brothers believed in (Jesus)."* (John 7:5) His family lived with Jesus for 30 years and still didn't understand. Not one of Jesus's brothers was a disciple before His crucifixion. But after His resurrection and ascension, we find them in the upper room as believers. In Acts 1:14 we see that *"They all met together and were constantly united in prayer, along with Mary the mother of Jesus, several other women, and the brothers of Jesus."*

God never gives up on people, which means we should never give up on our family. We are called to reach our family members. Even when it's a challenge, even when it's difficult, even when it seems no one is listening. You never know what one thing will be that final thing that gets their attention. So always be kind, loving, truthful, and patient…and never give up!

The third way God appoints you as a follower of Jesus is to reach your world. I attended a special gathering of pastors this past week. It was a gathering of men and women who are leading in some of the most impactful churches across our country. It was a refreshing time of encouragement, challenge, and inspiration.

But the most impactful part for me was hearing story after story of how God is currently using normal, everyday people in phenomenal ways across our country. A common theme that resonates strongly with these leaders, is the story of how everyday believers are stepping up and stepping out for the Kingdom of God in churches all across America.

Many of the pastors I spoke with shared about the people of their congregation and shared how their greatest joy in ministry is not the sermon, but rather it's when a follower of Christ begins to serve. "Seeing the church be the church is my greatest joy in ministry," one pastor told me. I echo the sentiment.

I want to impress upon your heart today just how much God has appointed you to serve. For most of you, it will be something in connection to our church and community. For others, it will be an appointment connected to something further away.

Maybe God is calling you to the mission field. Maybe God is calling you to further your education in preparation for pastoring or some other full-time ministry role. Whatever God is calling you to do, go do it. He's appointed you! Don't wait any longer. God has set you aside to do His work. Step into that calling and step out of your comfort zone.

The first thing God does when He appoints you is He Retains you. Next, He Renames you...

WHEN GOD RENAMES YOU

In the second part of our "3:16 Story," we see that Simon had his name changed to Peter. *"And (Jesus) appointed the Twelve; and to Simon He added the name Peter."* (Mark 3:16 BLB) What's the significance of this? Why did Jesus do that?

In the Bible, names carried far more significance than our modern names do. Changes such as Abram to Abraham, or Saul to Paul indicate a transformation in the person's life, beyond just a preferred sound, trend, or family tradition. Biblical names had a deeper meaning and a name change often signaled a significant shift in the person's life. That's what happened to Peter after he was appointed by Jesus to follow Him.

Simon means "a hearing" while Peter means a "rock." This was a much better description in relation to what Jesus was about to do in his life. It was Peter who first proclaimed Jesus as *"The Christ, the Son of the living God."* (Matthew 16:16) This very confession is the Truth upon which the Church is built. Peter was eventually considered a leader among the apostles and carried a significant weight of that calling. He was in many ways a rock to the early Christian movement.

This idea of Simon Peter getting a new name is symbolic as it relates to a believer becoming a new creation when they follow Jesus. The Bible reminds us, *"Therefore, if anyone is in Christ, he is a new creation. The old has passed away; behold, the new has come"* (2 Corinthians 5:17)

So, this brings up a great question…When God makes us a new creation what kind of changes do we see? How does God "Rename" us?

Our identity, desires, and nature all change once the Holy Spirit resides in the heart of a believer. Look how Paul describes it in one of his letters to the Christians in Ephesus.

"[2]You used to live in sin, just like the rest of the world…[3]All of us used to live that way, following the passionate desires and inclinations of our sinful nature…[4]But God is so rich in mercy, and He loved us so much…[5]He gave us life…[10]He has created us anew in Christ Jesus, so we can do the good things He planned for us long ago." (Ephesians 2:2-10)

How does your identity change? Before you become a Christian the world wants to identify you by what you've done. You're this or you're that. You've done this, or this was done to you, therefore, you've been labeled something unimaginable. Something you never wanted.

People struggle every day with this issue of identity. We live in a culture of chaotic identities.

In his book, *True Identity*, author John Majors writes, "Understanding your identity is important because who you are determines what you do. You will act like who you are. And the more you intentionally shape your identity, the more your actions will reflect the person you want to be. Having a clear sense of identity is having integrity; meaning, you act, live, and think in a way that matches the way you view yourself. But if you don't have that, it creates confusion, chaos, and inner turmoil. And it can feed an identity crisis."[18]

The Bible teaches us that through Jesus we have an identity rooted in Him. We have an identity based upon whom God says that I am, not what those around me say. My identity is not based on what I've done or what has been done to me. My identity is secure in what Christ has already done for me on the cross.

Part of our problem is thinking too much about our identity and not enough about God. Instead of asking what's my identity, a better question would be, what is God's identity and where do I fit in His story?

I have value because God counts me as valuable. I have worth because God says I am worth rescuing. Once we get that into our core, into the inside of our hearts and mind, there is nothing that can shake us. Nothing that can move us. Nothing that can prevent us from living our life in a way that truly honors God.

How do your desires change? Before Jesus all of us were held captive to desires and appetites unhealthy for our spiritual life. We wanted to go places and see people that were not helping our life get better. We knew these places, people, and habits were not good for us, but somehow we were trapped in a vicious loop of behavior and patterns that brought our life down.

For some, the pain and price of those desires cost you dearly. For others, you're either feeling the effects of those desires today or about to shortly and you're looking for a way out.

- How do I escape this trap of addiction?

- How do I sever this cycle of compulsion?

- How do I end this series of emptiness and pain in my life?

When you've come to a place where the emptiness of your desires has left you with a hole in the center of your soul, there's only one person who can fill that emptiness. His name is Jesus. The brilliant 17th-century philosopher and mathematician Blaise Pascal once noted,

"What else does this craving, and this helplessness, proclaim but that there was once in man a true happiness, of which all that now remains is the empty print and trace? This he tries in vain to fill with everything around him, seeking in things that are not there the help he cannot find in those that are, though none can help, since this infinite abyss can be filled only with an infinite and immutable object; in other words, by God himself."[19]

How does your nature change? To comprehend this "new creation," we must recognize it as a creation of God brought about by His will (John 1:13). It is not inherited from our parents or self-made, but rather, a completely new and unique creation by God, just as the universe was created ex nihilo (out of nothing) so you receive a new nature out of nothing.

The old things in us, including natural pride, love of sin, reliance on works, and most significantly, the love of self and self-justification, have passed away. This is because the new creation looks to Christ, not self, and the old nature was crucified along with our sin.

With the passing of the old nature, the new nature has come. The old, lifeless things are replaced by new, vibrant things that reflect God's glory. The new soul rejoices in God. Our outlook, emotions, wishes, and comprehension are new and unique. We view the world with fresh eyes. The Bible becomes a newly discovered book, and we marvel at its beauty that we previously overlooked.

Our nature is transformed, and we are connected to a new world. We see the universe as being filled with new wonders that glorify God. Our attitudes toward others change—we feel a new kind of love for family and friends, compassion for enemies, and love for all humanity. We discard our old ways and adopt a new self, created in God's likeness and righteousness.

Here's how the Bible describes it:

"You've gotten rid of the person you used to be and the life you used to live." (Colossians 3:9 GNT)

"Put on your new nature, created to be like God—truly righteous and holy." (Ephesians 4:24)

Now that we've learned that God appoints us by first Retaining us and then by Renaming us, what's the third way God appoints us?

WHEN GOD RECLAIMS YOU

This third point is going to hit home with some of you on a very personal level. Here's what I mean by that; even though we know God has Retained us (meaning He's called us to Himself), and even though we know that God has Renamed us (meaning He's changed us), sometimes we fail, and fall short of God's best for our life.

The question then becomes…

- What happens when you lose your way?

- What happens when you lose your first love?

- What happens when you question your calling?

It doesn't matter if you're a church attender or even a pastor, missionary or Christian leader, the reality of being tempted to move backward in your faith is present every day. But I want to encourage you to know that God never lets you go. If you've moved backward in your faith, if you feel like you're not on fire like you use to be, know that God gets it and He's coming back for you. He's coming to Reclaim you!

Because Peter is the pivotal figure in this chapter's "3:16 Story", I want to extend our lesson to include what happened to him three years after his appointment from Jesus along the pebbled shores of the Sea of Galilee.

Imagine the journey Peter took after he decided to follow Jesus. He went from an everyday fisherman to a traveling missionary. He saw blind people see again. He witnessed the sick be made well. He watched Jesus as He confronted the religious leaders of his day. He saw lame men walk. He saw dead people raised to life. He experienced walking on water, viewing a transfiguration, the feeding of 5,000, and many other miraculous events.

Yet even with all of this first-hand supernatural experience, Peter (like many of us) went backward. He lost his spiritual edge and ultimately, he denied Christ. Not just once or twice, but three times within a very short time span.

The Bible tells us that after Jesus was arrested and put on trial,

Peter was confronted by a servant girl just outside the courthouse. Because of fear, Peter denied that he knew Jesus, and soon after, remorse and guilt flooded his heart. Three days later Peter raced to the empty tomb and was overjoyed when he discovered that Jesus had indeed risen from the dead.

But there's more to the story. According to the Gospel of John, even though Jesus appeared to Peter after the resurrection something still needed to be done.

In chapter twenty-one we find Peter and some other disciples fishing on the Sea of Galilee. Peter had gone back to his old way of life. But Jesus wasn't finished with Peter. He called out to Peter and the other disciples from the shore. Peter recognized the voice of Jesus and jumped in the water and quickly swam back to Him. Jesus welcomed him and they sat down for breakfast. During their time together, Jesus asked Peter three times if he loved Him. All three times Peter said, "Yes, of course I love you."

Some have speculated that it wasn't Jesus who needed to hear Peter say he loved Him three times, but rather it was Peter who needed to hear it for himself. Once for each of his three denials…only days before. At the conclusion of the conversation, Jesus simply says, "Follow Me" to Peter…again! (John 21:19)

Did you catch that? These are the same two words Jesus told Peter at the very beginning, "Follow Me" (Mark 1:17). What's happening here? It's simple, Jesus is reminding Peter that he's still called. He's still appointed. Jesus is not going to leave Peter to his old ways, just because he messed up a few times. No, that's not how God works. He's directing Peter to reclaim the calling God had on his life.

Some of you need to do that today. Don't quit on what God has for you. God hasn't quit on you, so don't quit on yourself. When you walk away from your calling God doesn't walk away from you, instead...

- He recalls you

- He reengages with you

- He re-appoints you

- He reclaims you

"For (God) called you to share in His Kingdom and glory." (1 Thessalonians 2:12)

"God is faithful, by Whom you were called into the fellowship of His Son, Jesus Christ our Lord." (1 Corinthians 1:9)

I mentioned to you earlier that I was a part of a meeting with a group of pastors and ministry leaders from around the country. In one of the meetings, this discussion of calling and being appointed by God for a task or duty was brought up. To me, the most memorable comment that was shared with the group was simply, "sometimes the most spiritual thing you can do is just show up!" In other words, don't run from your calling, run to it. Don't walk away from your calling, walk with it. Don't hide from your calling, go pursue it.

Jesus showed up on that historic morning and Peter thought the meeting was about breakfast. But that's not what Jesus had in mind. Jesus had one goal in mind and that was to get Peter back on track and He did.

But how about you? Have you jumped the track in your

relationship with God? Were you once in a better place with God? A place where things were going great. But now, you've messed up, grown cold or lost your spiritual edge? When God appoints you the first time, it's a calling that stays with you. God doesn't change His mind about your calling. He doesn't say, "Oh, I guess I messed that one up. I guess I shouldn't have appointed that one, he's a flake." That's not how it works.

The Bible teaches us, *"For the gifts and the calling of God are irrevocable."* (Romans 11:29) This means God has already decided on you. In His infinite wisdom, He's already determined that He wants you on His team. That's not going to change. No matter what you do or don't do. It's a fixed deal. It's not based on your actions; it's based on His character.

When you do something like Peter and walk away or climb back into the old life, your old ways, God's not going to leave you there. He's coming after you. Because His calling is irrevocable, irreversible, unalterable, unchangeable, fixed, final, and finished. It was decided upon before you were even born. In God's foreknowledge of your life, He's already seen the before, during, and after of every situation. He decided to love you anyway.

So come back to Jesus today. Quit hanging out feeling down, depressed, and disappointed. Jump out of that boat and get with Jesus and do it now. He's not going to reject you. He's going to embrace you and reinstate you. He's appointed you.

CONCLUSION

In keeping with our theme, we are learning one new attribute of God in each one of our "3:16 Stories." The attribute (or character trait) we learn about in Mark 3:16 is God's Wisdom.

Pastor and theologian A.W. Tozer once wrote, "Wisdom, among other things, is the ability to devise perfect ends and to achieve those ends by the most perfect means. It sees the end from the beginning, so there can be no need to guess or conjecture. Wisdom sees everything in focus, each in proper relation to all, and is thus able to work toward predestined goals with flawless precision."[20]

This is how God sees the world. His view is much higher than this world. He flies above the universe and transcends time and space. His knowledge and understanding is not like ours. He doesn't process a thing. He doesn't contemplate a thing. He doesn't guess at a thing. God decrees something and then in His wisdom, it's worked out in and through our lives.

The fact that God can never be wiser means He is always doing the wisest thing in our lives. No plan we could make for our lives could be better than the plan He has already crafted and is carrying out for us. We might not understand His ways today, but we can trust that because God is infinitely wise, He truly is working all things out in the best possible way.[21]

That's why I want to encourage you to fully walk in the truth that you serve a God who appoints you. And when you connect your life to that calling, sit back and watch the fireworks, because it's going to be spectacular.

So how did Hal Donaldson get from Calcutta to Forbes during the past 33 years?

Donaldson returned home from India with a changed perspective. He knew he needed to do something to help his fellow man. But what? That's when he says God gave him an idea. He packed up his car and hit the road. He traveled to eight cities in America and stayed on the streets for three nights in each of them. He spent that time talking with the people he encountered. People who were homeless, people who had turned to prostitution, and those struggling with addiction. He listened to their stories. "My heart broke," he says. "I knew I could no longer just live for myself."

Inspired by Mother Teresa's words and the stories he'd heard across America, Donaldson loaded a pick-up truck with $300 worth of groceries. He drove around Northern California handing them out to anyone who looked like they needed help. As word got around about his endeavors, his operation grew bigger. "It grew from a pick-up truck to a box truck to a semi-truck to warehouses," he said. In 1994, Donaldson created the nonprofit organization, Convoy of Hope.

Today, Convoy of Hope works with communities across America and around the world—from India to South Africa, Bulgaria to Nicaragua. Their work focuses on feeding children, women's empowerment, helping farmers, and disaster services.

Donaldson says the response from people helped by Convoy of Hope is powerful. "People said we've shown them there was still good," he says. "That we've given them hope." But perhaps even more profound was the response from people who joined their operation, driven by their need to help others. "People said they didn't know what to do, but then they heard about us,"

Donaldson says. "We underestimate what we can accomplish. I experienced poverty but I experienced kindness. It can transform lives. God wants to help the poor and He's looking for people who are willing."[22]

When you meet Hal, you instantly know you've met a man who's walking in his divine calling. Stop worrying about what you've done or what you've missed out on. Start moving forward into what God has for you and your specific calling. Every day you wait is another day of blessing that marches right by you. Are you ready to embrace your calling today?

Chapter 4

The God Who Loves You

John 3:16

Attribute: God is Love

In 2009, quarterback Tim Tebow prepared himself for college football's National Championship game. He said God led him to write John 3:16 under his eyes for all the world to see, "God kept bringing to my heart this verse which is the essence of Christianity. It's the essence of our hope." After winning the game Tebow heard that 94 million people Googled the famous Bible verse. "I was just so humbled by how big God is," he said. But that's not where the story ends.

In 2012, precisely 3 years later, now as a Denver Bronco, Tebow found himself playing QB against the Pittsburgh Steelers in the NFL playoffs. After the Broncos won, he headed into the post-game press conference. His public relations representative stopped him in his tracks. "He says, 'Timmy, did you realize what happened?' I was like, 'Yeah, we just beat the Steelers. We're going to play the Patriots.' And he was like, 'No, do you realize what happened?'"

"He said, 'During the game, you threw for 316 yards, your yards per completion were 31.6, your yards per rush were 3.16, the ratings for the night were 31.6, and the time of possession was 31.06 and during the game, 91 million people Googled John 3:16 and it's the number one trending thing on every platform.'"

Tebow believes God did something miraculous that night, "I just have to be willing to step out and say, 'Here you go, God, I'm going to give you my fish and my loaves of bread and watch what He does with it.'"[23]

Sometimes God likes to surprise us, doesn't He? Something about this verse speaks to us. Something in this verse connects to the deepest part of our human experience.

There's little doubt that John 3:16 is the most popular verse in the Bible. It has been printed on more bumper stickers, t-shirts, and hats, as well as written on more faces, fabric, and posterboards than any other verse. But what makes this small verse so popular?

Maybe because it's easy to remember due to sheer repetition. Perhaps there's a message sent from God to each of us. A message that resonates deep within us when we read it.

In this "3:16 Story," you will discover four things about God's love that will transform your life. Four surprising elements of God's love that will help you overcome your situation, crush your problems, and overthrow your fears.

Here it is, *"For God so loved the world, that He gave His only Son, that whoever believes in Him should not perish but have eternal life." (John 3:16)*

The first thing we learn is...

GOD'S LOVE IS UNIVERSAL

"For God so loved the world, that He gave His only Son, that whoever believes in Him should not perish but have eternal life." (John 3:16)

I remember being on an airplane a few years ago and when the person sitting next to me found out I was a pastor, the conversation turned to spiritual matters. During the conversation, I shared John 3:16 with him. He wanted to know the most powerful or convincing verse in the Bible. So I shared with him this famous passage.

As I began sharing, he stopped me after the "for God so loved the world" part and asked, "Why does God love the world? If I was God, I certainly wouldn't love this world. It's full of messed up people and hypocrites. People treat each other in horrible ways, what's there to love about it?"

I always thought that was an interesting observation. I can see how someone would be led to that conclusion if they didn't know God or understand His nature. C.S. Lewis once noted, "God loved us not because we were lovable, but because He is love."

Part of God's nature is that He loves because that's who He is. In other words, God cannot do anything other than love. It's like asking you to stop being a human. You can't do that because it's who you are.

It's not only important to remember God is love, but that His love is universal. That means His love is for everyone. No one can corner the market on God's love even though many have tried and will continue to try. The Bible tells us God's love is for the entire world. He reveals that love to us through the pages of the Bible.

This carries with it a few implications.

The first is that God's love is universal in terms of geography. That means there isn't a certain area of the planet, country, or people group that God loves more or less than somewhere else. We act like that, but God doesn't. Many people set another person's value based on income, social status, race, nationality, or country of origin, but God doesn't. According to the Bible, we are all part of one race, the human race. God wants everyone to come to a place of repentance and a right relationship with Him.

The second is that God's love is universal in its application. When the Bible says God loves the world, it's not saying that God loves all the elements found in the world. He doesn't love it when people hurt each other. God doesn't love it when we do things contrary to His will. God's love is universal in that His love can be applied to all our situations in helping bring us back to Him.

According to one writer, the point of God's love for the world… "is not to suggest that the world is so big that it takes a great deal of love to embrace it all, but that the world is so bad that it takes a great kind of love to love it at all, and much more to love it as God has loved it when He gave His Son for it."[24]

No matter where you find yourself today, God's love will find you. The Bible reminds us, *"Nothing in all creation will ever be able to separate us from the love of God that is revealed in Christ*

Jesus our Lord." (Romans 8:39)

Not only is God's love Universal but…

GOD'S LOVE IS UNMERITED

"For God so loved the world that He gave His only Son, that whoever believes in Him should not perish but have eternal life." (John 3:16) (1 John 4:9-10)

This word unmerited means "undeserved" or "unearned." Have you ever received something you didn't earn? It may have been a present from someone special. Maybe it was a bonus at work. Maybe you had a teacher who gave you extra credit or graded your work with a higher mark than you deserved. Hopefully, you've been blessed by receiving something beneficial when you didn't deserve it. That's what the Bible is saying here with God giving us His Son.

When God gave us Jesus, we didn't deserve it. Not a chance. Humanity has been messed up from the start. When Adam and Eve disobeyed God, the Bible tells us sin entered the world. The world was broken. We've been experiencing this brokenness ever since. But God didn't want to leave us in a condition of brokenness. He wanted to rescue us. So, He sent His Son to redeem us. Here's how the Bible describes it: *"But God showed His great love for us by sending Christ to die for us while we were still sinners."* (Romans 5:8)

You have value to God. You're worth rescuing! Never forget that. You may feel like you're a million miles away from God.

Something happened to you. You got caught up in something. Life hasn't turned out in a way that honors God and you know it. You're ashamed, confused, and devastated and you want to get real with God, but you don't know what to do. You feel like someone hijacked your future and you want to get it back.

A few years ago, there was a true story about a man in New York City who was kidnapped. His kidnappers called his wife and asked for a $100,000 ransom. The wife talked them down to $30,000.

The story had a positive conclusion: the man returned home unharmed, the money was recovered, and the kidnappers were caught and sent to jail. Yet, I kind of wonder what happened when the man got home and found out that his wife got him back for a discount.

Imagine what the negotiations must have been like: "$100,000 for that guy? You have got to be crazy. Just look at him. Plus, he's out of shape. You want $100,000? Not gonna happen. $30,000 is my top offer. Take it or leave it."

I feel for this guy. But in a way it's true for all of us, isn't it. At some point, we come to the realization that we're not as cool as we think we are. Not the "captain of industry" we thought we were. We're not as popular, prestigious, or prominent as we'd like to think.

Life has a way of flattening our egos and taking us down a few notches. Yet if we're not careful we can find ourselves in a place of thinking we are of little to no value.

Somewhere between a destructive ego and self-pity, we need

to find the rhythm of healthy self-awareness in our day-to-day existence. But even in that healthy space, we come to the realization there's nothing we can do to demand, mandate, or require God's love. After all, we're all broken, just in different places.

This is where the love of God kicks in. The kind of love that gives. "For God so loved...He gave."

This kind of love, the kind of love God gives is called "selfless love" or "sacrificial love." That's the word used here in John 3:16 in the original language.

During Jesus' day, there were four different ways to describe love. It's kind of like our day. We might say, "I love the 49ers," or "I love my dog," or "I love my wife and kids." Each one of these statements carries a different level of love. It was the same way during Jesus' day.

Yet instead of one-word meaning different things, they had four different words to portray the kind of love they were describing. Here they are; Storge, Phileo, Eros, and Agape.[25]

Storge – Love for your family

- Noah and his family (Genesis 6-9)
- The siblings Mary, Martha, and Lazarus of Bethany (Luke 10; John 11)

Phileo – Love for your friends

- David and Jonathan (1 Samuel 18)
- Paul and Timothy (Acts 16:1-3; Acts 17:14-15)

Eros – Love for your husband/wife

73

- Part of a father's instruction to his son (Prov 5:18-20)

- The King and his bride (Song of Solomon)

Agape – Sacrificial Love

- Between God and us (John 3:16; Romans 8:38-39)

- Between us and the Lord (John 13:34-35)

- Between us and others (1 John 3:16)

Agape love is what the Bible is talking about in this "3:16 Story." Agape love is known for being the highest form of affection. It's sacrificial and selfless love. Jesus talked about this one time with His disciples when He said, *"Greater love has no one than this, that someone lay down his life for his friends."* (John 15:13) The word for love here is "agape."

Putting this all together, you're seeing a picture here of God sending Jesus in a sacrificial way to redeem you because of His "agape" love for you. All of this is done though we don't deserve it. That's unmerited love. Undeserved. Unwarranted. Unearned.

We've seen God's love as being Universal and Unmerited, next we discover...

GOD'S LOVE IS UNCONDITIONAL

"For God so loved the world, that He gave His only Son, that whoever believes in Him should not perish but have eternal life." (John 3:16)

Our "3:16 Story" goes on to say that when you believe in Jesus something happens. We will get to what happens in just a minute, but first what does it mean to "believe in Him" and who's included in this invite?

"Whoever" means exactly what it says, that's anyone, including you. And the only qualification for receiving the benefit is to believe. More specifically, believe in "Him" (Jesus).

Someone asked me if whoever actually means whoever, or does it mean something like… "whoever goes to church," or "whoever grew up in a Christian home," or "whoever has special 'God access' in their life?"

I don't know what special "God access" is, but…yes, it literally means whoever, all, or everyone. It's the most inclusive way to say it. There is nothing exclusionary about God's love. You and I need to understand this. Look at this verse in Paul's letter to Timothy.

"God wants everyone to be saved and to know the whole truth." (1 Timothy 2:4 CEV) You see this same word everyone being used here too.

Being inclusive starts with God. Inclusivity isn't a modern term created within our generation. As if pop psychology or gender studies programs stumbled onto some great unheard-of concept. All this talk about equity, diversity, and inclusion begins with God. But the world corrupts it and pits people against people. One tribe against another tribe. You can see it play out in our society. It's all over social media, in the news, and it drives much of the political discourse of our day.

We shouldn't take the bait. We need to rise above all the noise and focus the conversations on what matters and that's an individual's relationship with God. In this regard, we are all on the same playing field. It's equal ground at the foot of the cross. Real diversity, inclusion, and equity start from a spiritual perspective. Once we align our life with God then we will treat each other the way God does, equally.

Looking back to 1 Timothy 2:4, the Bible is clearly teaching that everyone is invited to be saved and then live out (or to know) the truth. That means living out the way of Jesus to the world. In other words we don't clean up to take a bath. We come to Jesus just as we are, messed up, mixed up, and torn up. He fixes us, restores us, and remakes us. He puts our feet on solid ground. He provides a new way, a better way to live our life based upon the original Creation and design for our life and all our relationships in life.

Look how the Psalmist describes it, *"¹I waited patiently for the LORD to help me, and He turned to me and heard my cry. 2He lifted me out of the pit of despair, out of the mud and the mire. He set my feet on solid ground and steadied me as I walked along. 3He has given me a new song to sing, a hymn of praise to our God. Many will see what He has done and be amazed. They will put their trust in the LORD."* (Psalms 40:1-3)

We tend to place the clean-up part first and when we do, we've got it backward. God's love is unconditional, no matter where you find yourself today, God loves you and wants you to walk in the truth. His design for your life is far better than anything you can fathom.

The question then arises, what does it mean to believe? Does it simply mean to believe Jesus existed? Does it mean to agree with the fact that Jesus was a historical figure, like saying that I believe in Abraham Lincoln? Or does it mean something far greater?

The original word used here is pisteuo (pist-yoo'-o) and means to place your trust in someone. It means to have confidence in the person to carry out what they say they can do. You trust the bank to keep your money. You trust the surgeon to stitch you back together again. You trust the engineers of an airplane that they designed and built it properly so that it doesn't drop out of the sky. We trust in people all the time.

The famous performer Charles Blondin made headlines in the summer of 1859 with his death-defying walks across Niagara Falls on a tightrope stretching a quarter of a mile across. The thundering sound of the pounding water was so loud that it drowned out all other sounds, but still, Blondin managed to walk back and forth between Canada and the United States, 160 feet above the falls. The crowds on both sides watched in shock and awe as he performed various feats, including crossing blindfolded while pushing a wheelbarrow.

His bravery and skill earned him a reputation as one of the greatest tightrope walkers of all time. He crossed the Falls several times, each time with a different challenge. He crossed the Falls in a sack, on stilts, on a bicycle, and even cooked an omelet while crossing. The crowd would "Ooooh" and "Aaaah" as they watched him perform each stunt, but it was after pushing the wheelbarrow across while blindfolded that Blondin asked for audience participation.

He asked the crowd if they believed he could carry a person across in the wheelbarrow, and of course, the crowd shouted yes.

But when he posed the question, "Who will get in the wheelbarrow?" no one volunteered.26

Although the love of God is unconditional toward us, we can only experience this great love as we completely trust in Jesus 100%. Have you done that yet? Have you jumped into the wheelbarrow with God? Don't be a fan shouting on the sidelines, be the one who gets in and says, "I'm with you all the way Jesus. It's me and you, let's roll!"

So far, we've seen God's love is Universal, Unmerited, and Unconditional. Finally, we discover...

GOD'S LOVE IS UNENDING

"For God so loved the world, that He gave His only Son, that whoever believes in Him should not perish but have eternal life." (John 3:16)

A man once observed a young boy in a field flying a kite. He noticed that there was something odd about the way the boy was standing and holding on to the string. He walked up to the boy and then learned that the boy was blind. He said, "Do you like flying kites?"

The boy said, "I sure do." The man was curious and asked, "How's that, when you can't see it?" The boy answered, "I may not be able to see it, but I can feel it tugging!" Like the little boy, God's eternal love tugs at our hearts and lets us know He's there.

The Bible tells us, *"He has planted eternity in the human heart."* (Ecclesiastes 3:11)

Over 80% of Americans still believe in God and sense this spiritual reality in life.[27] You've probably asked yourself the question, what happens to me when I die? Where do I go? You're not alone in asking or sensing there is something beyond this life. The Bible describes it as an eternity.

I once rode my motorcycle to Tombstone, Arizona and while there I visited the famous Boot Hill cemetery. I saw a late 1800s epitaph for a bank teller named Lester Moore.

It read:

> Here lies Lester Moore
> Four slugs from a .44
> No Les No More

It reminded me of another epitaph from Thurmont, Maryland:

> Here lies an Atheist
> All dressed up
> And no place to go

In both cases, the humor is fantastic, but the theology is horribly wrong. According to the Bible, when we die we enter eternity. We go somewhere. According to our "3:16 Passage," when we believe in Jesus we won't "perish" but instead "have eternal life."

"Perish" means to be eternally separated from God with no way to get back. It's over, it's done, it's settled. The Bible calls this location hell. "Eternal life" means to be with God forever and to enjoy all the blessings and benefits of heaven in the presence of God.

Some people ask, "Why does God send people to hell?" He

doesn't. According to the Bible, God doesn't want anyone to "perish." In fact, it is against His will that anyone should perish. Unfortunately, people choose to exist apart from God and that's becoming more evident in our culture today. When you reject God you are setting yourself up for an eternity without Him.

God provides you with a better way.

I heard a story about a little girl who misquoted John 3:16 as "whoever believes in Him should not perish but have internal life." She got one word mistaken, but her theology is faultless. When we say God's love is unending that doesn't mean you have to wait until Heaven to begin experiencing it.

Philippians 1:21 tells us, *"To live is Christ, and to die is gain."* John 10:10 reminds us, *"I came that they may have life and have it abundantly."*

In his book, *God Loves You*, Pastor David Jeremiah describes it this way: "John 3:16 tells an amazing love story, doesn't it? It begins with God, who has no beginning and concludes with life that has no ending. That's life with no limits, and it can begin now. Think of it: no limits to joy, no limits to kingdom service, and no limits to how much we will come to resemble His Son as we grow more like Him every day."[28]

Are you starting to see John 3:16 in a different light? You don't have to wait until you die to begin experiencing eternal life. As a follower of Jesus, your eternal life has already begun.

Do you know why we have John 3:16? It's because of a man named Nicodemus. He was a Jewish ruler who came to Jesus privately at night. He didn't want everyone to know he was curious about Jesus and who He really was. He was concerned with his social standing. On that night Jesus explained to Nicodemus what it means to experience the fullness of God's love. Toward the end of his discussion, Jesus provided him what Martin Luther calls the miniature gospel, and what we know as John 3:16.

But whatever happened to the man who first heard this famous passage? Did he say yes to following Jesus? Not at first, but in John 19:38-42 we learn that Nicodemus and one other person prepared Jesus' body for burial. Nicodemus eventually said yes. And Church history tells us that Nicodemus was eventually martyred in the first century for his Christian faith.

How about you? Have you said yes to the invitation of Jesus? If not, you can do that today.

In sum, God's love is Universal, Unmerited, Unconditional, and Unending. Ultimately, God's love is amazing.

CONCLUSION

Throughout this book, we've tracked in parallel with each "3:16 Story" a specific attribute of God. We've been asking, what does this "3:16 verse" tell us about one of God's character qualities or His nature? Undoubtedly this particular verse has the easiest attribute to identify. It's the attribute of Love.

When we say God is Love what we mean by that is…

- God is **Active**. He is pulling us to Himself in a way that is personal and connective.
- God is **Open**. He is transparent in His motive, desire,

and will.

- God is **Stable**. His love is eternal, sovereign, unchanging, and infinite.

You can't love on empty. You run out of niceness when you rely on your own strength. You need to draw from an unlimited well. God's well.

As you read this chapter, I believe the authenticity of God's love has **connected** to you deep in your heart. Why is that? This attribute of God's Love is exactly what our generation is longing for. We live in a time where...

- The rate of the fatherless has skyrocketed.[29]

- The rate of disconnected people continues to grow.

- The rate of divorce has yet to slow down.

- Family relationships are at their breaking point.

Many of you are hanging on by a thread. One wrong statement, one misunderstood comment...and whatever small or fragile connection there is... will be cut. People are living on relational fumes. You need help. You need God's help. You need the safety and stability of your heavenly Father to rescue you.

God can only save a culture by saving individuals. God can only save your family by saving you first. That's how it works.

One hundred years have passed since the sinking of the Titanic which claimed the lives of over 1,500 passengers. One of the most remarkable stories is that of John Harper, a pastor and preacher who was on board with his six-year-old daughter. Harper, from

London, was enroute to Chicago to preach at Moody Church. He was slated to become the next pastor.

When the Titanic hit the iceberg, Harper led his daughter to a lifeboat, but instead of following her, he chose to use his last moments to share the gospel with as many people as possible. He ran from person to person, offering them the chance to know Christ. As the ship began to sink, he shouted, "Women, children, and the unsaved into the lifeboats." Despite the danger, Harper continued to preach the gospel until the very end, even as he struggled through hypothermia to reach as many people as he could.

Four years after the tragedy, a survivor testified at a meeting in Ontario, Canada about his encounter with Harper in the icy waters of the Atlantic. Harper had approached him twice, inviting him to believe in Jesus, and finally, the man gave his life to Christ just before Harper lost his life to the frozen water. This man became the last convert of John Harper.

When the Titanic set sail there were descriptions of three classes of passengers. The tragedy of the Titanic reminds us there are only two classes of people: those who know Christ and will spend eternity with God in Heaven, and those who do not.

The owners of the Titanic placed a board outside their office in Liverpool, England after the tragedy, reading, "KNOWN TO BE SAVED" and "KNOWN TO BE LOST," reaffirming the truth that John Harper already knew.[30]

How about you? If God had a board in Heaven that read, Known to be Saved and Known to be Lost, which board would your name be on?

I want you to do something with me. I want you to personalize John 3:16.

Here it is,

For God so loved **the world**, that He gave His only Son, that whoever believes in Him should not perish but have eternal life

For God so loved_____(your name)_____, that He gave His only Son, that if_____(your name)_____, believes in Him should not perish but have eternal life.

Chapter 5

The God Who Heals You

Acts 3:16

Attribute: God is Good

Have you ever needed medical attention due to an illness? Perhaps you've visited a doctor for a cold, been hospitalized, or are currently managing a chronic illness or disability.

US Healthcare costs exceeded $4 trillion in 2022, making it the highest amount ever recorded for a country.[31] This number has grown four times since 2000 and shows no indication of slowing down. Good health is a top priority for many.

The question remains, why do we spend close to 20% of our total economic production on healthcare? The simple answer is that it's no fun to be sick. It feels horrible. Being healthy is a much more favorable way to live.

When I preached the sermon this chapter is based on, I had my arm in a sling. Not because I had injured it, but because I was illustrating a point. That is, when you see someone who is injured, it's easy to notice them and when we see a person who is hurting, we instinctively want to help them become better. Why? Because we know how it feels. We have empathy for them.

In fact, many people felt sorry for me when they saw me walk out with my arm in a sling. Many probably wondered what happened to me. Some may have felt a pain in their arm when they saw me. That's called mirror-touch synesthesia (sĭn″ĭs-thē′zhə). It's a matching of the pain you see in someone else.

In this chapter, we discover that God is a God who heals.

In "Acts 3:16" we read, *"Through faith in the name of Jesus, this man was healed—and you know how crippled he was before. Faith in Jesus' name has healed him before your very eyes."* (Acts 3:16)

In the story, Peter and John decide to go to church for a time of prayer at 3 o'clock in the afternoon. When they arrive at church, there's a man the Bible describes as lame. That means he was crippled. He couldn't walk and was dependent on family or friends to carry him to a high-traffic place where he could beg for money from those passing by.

When Peter and John walked by the man, he asked for a donation. Let's see what happened, *"⁶Peter said, 'I have no silver and gold, but what I do have I give to you. In the name of Jesus Christ of Nazareth, rise up and walk!' ⁷And He took him by the right hand and raised him up, and immediately his feet and ankles were made strong. ⁸And leaping up, he stood and began to walk, and entered the temple with them, walking and leaping and praising God."* (Acts 3:6-8)

A miraculous event occurred when this man, who had been born crippled and begging for help for 40 years, was finally healed. Healed by someone who gave him something far more valuable than money.

Maybe you are not physically crippled, but instead injured emotionally, relationally, or spiritually. This struggle may be recent for you, while others may feel like they've been dealing with it for 40 years or even longer. If you're hurting, I want to share with you that there's hope!

In this chapter we will discover three things about how God uses healing to reveal His nature and help us recognize our deep need for Him.

The first thing we discover is…

THE REALITY OF DIVINE HEALING

"Through faith in the name of Jesus, this man was healed—and you know how crippled he was before. Faith in Jesus' name has healed him before your very eyes." (Acts 3:16)

It's not uncommon for a pastor to field questions about divine healing. Many people ask, "Does God still heal people as He did in the Bible?" Other questions about who God heals, why doesn't He heal, and why we pray for healing are asked as well. These are good questions and are often sincere.

There's zero doubt Jesus performed many miracles in the New Testament. In His time on planet earth, it's recorded in the Gospel letters that He performed many miracles, healings, and wonders.

What's even more interesting is that the four Gospels of Matthew, Mark, Luke, and John cover only a portion of what Jesus accomplished. The last verse of the last Gospel tells us, *"Now there are also many other things that Jesus did. Were every one of them to be written, I suppose that the world itself could not contain the books that would be written."* (John 21:25)

There are over 40 miraculous events recorded about Jesus and the vast majority of these events were specifically related to someone or groups of individuals being healed.[32]

Following the resurrection and ascension of Jesus, the early church experienced God do miraculous things as well. One of these events is found in this "3:16 Story." Seven of the 29 miracles in the book of Acts deal with Jesus healing someone.[33]

Additionally,

- In Romans, Paul references his miraculous ministry to the Gentiles. (15:18-20)

- In Galatians, Paul asks about miracles performed in their midst. (3:1-5)

- In Philippians, Epaphroditus was healed by God. (2:25-30)

- In James, prayer for the sick is encouraged. (5:14-18)

- In 1 Peter, Christ is our healer. (2:24)

- In the Book of Revelations, there will be a healing of the nations. (22:2)

Embedded within the pages of the Bible is the idea of healing. Yet the question of whether divine healing happens today brings up various opinions.

Some Christian leaders teach that followers of Jesus will receive health and prosperity if they have enough faith. This puts a tremendous amount of pressure on Christians and is a spiritually unhealthy mindset. If all the pressure is on me to see God move, I think we're going about it all wrong. It's a misapplication of Scripture.

Skeptics, on the other hand, doubt the legitimacy of physical healing. They either think God doesn't exist, doesn't care, or that He stopped doing miraculous things after the time of Christ. The problem here is the evidence is just too strong in favor of God working in people's lives. Especially in ways that are miraculous. Craig Keener's[34] two-volume series "Miracles" is a phenomenal study of God's current and historical interactions with humanity across the globe. For those doubting the miraculous in today's world, it's a great place to start.

Lastly, Christians who acknowledge that God sometimes heals may still struggle with questions such as do they have enough faith for healing or whether their sickness is a gift from God.

To find an answer to this perplexity, it's essential to recognize the different types of what I call "God-designed" healings.[35]

God Design #1 is <u>natural</u> healing. This occurs through the body's natural process of eradicating sickness and repairing itself. For instance, when a virus invades the body, the white blood cells attack it. Additionally, the body constantly repairs itself by sending nutrients for consistent restoration year after year. This natural healing process is a manifestation of God's grace. He created this natural process of repair.

God Design #2 is a <u>miraculous</u> intervention. This occurs when God performs healing beyond the body's natural capabilities, such as restoring hearing or strengthening muscular, bone, or other tissue. These are the types of healings that people throughout the world continue to testify about. It's something beyond natural or medical explanation. People pray and God responds.

God Design #3 is through <u>medicine</u> and <u>science</u>. This is not to be overlooked or discounted by Christians. The availability of ambulances, expertise of medical professionals, and advancements in surgical techniques are all examples of the gracious gifts of God. He allows us to utilize our brains to share knowledge and wisdom as it relates to treatments and medicines.

God Design #4 is in <u>eternity</u>. The Bible calls this the resurrection of the dead where every physical disability is healed, and death is defeated. In this state, all corrupted bodies are transformed into incorruptible ones, free from sickness and affliction. Every physical disability, including deafness, damaged limbs, and blindness, is instantly healed. Conditions such as autism, Down syndrome, schizophrenia, and Alzheimer's disease are overcome in heaven. The only tears there will be tears of joy.

Understanding the different types of healing can help answer questions about God's healing, such as why healing may not always occur immediately, whether having faith is enough for healing, or whether sickness should be seen as a gift from God.

When you ask for healing, God may answer "Yes" or "Not yet" but as a Christian, through one of these four ways, God will ultimately provide healing for your physical body.

The Reality of Divine Healing brings us to our next discovery...

THE REALISM OF OUR HURTS

"Through faith in the name of Jesus, this man was healed— and you know how crippled he was before. Faith in Jesus' name has healed him before your very eyes." (Acts 3:16)

Getting back to our "3:16 Story," Peter stands before the skeptics of his day conveying the condition of this man prior to his healing. He was crippled at birth. He was unable to walk. He was broken. It appears the whole city knew of his condition. He was forty years old, and the Bible tells us he was brought to the center of town every day to beg for money. Everyone knew him and his story. It was a sad, regrettable, and hopeless story.

Yet the reality of this crippled man's condition reveals an inconvenient truth for all of us. We're not far from him because we're all broken, just in different places. If our human condition was a position of perfection, we wouldn't need healing, would we? We wouldn't need restoration. We wouldn't need a Savior. But we are all broken, and we all know it.

A fascinating construct of our culture is that we are less and less in need of immediate physical healing yet we invest more and more resources in medical care, more than any society in the history of humanity. We have become masterful at patching up our physical wounds, curing long-term diseases, and elongating the physicality of life. But on the inside we are more broken than ever.

Singer and songwriter Dave Matthews, one of the biggest-grossing live performers in history, speaks to the brokenness of our generation in one of his most famous lyrics:

The space between
The tears we cry is the laughter keeps us coming back for more
The space between
Our wicked lies where we hope to keep safe from pain.

If you're not familiar with the Dave Matthews Band, they hit the American pop culture scene in the early 1990s and sold more than 40 million copies of their music over the past 25 years. For Generation X, Matthew's music strikes a chord that resonates deep within the heart and soul of a hurting generation.

The generations to follow haven't fared much better. In a 2021 study Gen X, Millennials, and Gen Z, "May have advanced by leaps and bounds over the last century, but they are in worse health than their parents and grandparents were at their age. There has been a downhill slide over time: They reported more anxiety and depression symptoms, heavy drinking, and drug use. Recent years have seen a well-documented national rise in deaths from suicide, drug abuse, and problem drinking, which some experts have labeled "deaths of despair."[36]

What's happening in our culture? We're hurting. The breakdown of the family, the removal of biblical principles from schools, the rise of secularism in universities, and moral decay of the entertainment industry have sparked the match of despair which has lit the flame of a faceless abandonment of truth.

Like a violent wave crashing down upon the shores of future hope, loneliness is stripping away the vibrancy of the dreams of our youth. We're hurting, hopeless, broken. In many cases, we've been crippled from birth.

The realism of our hurts stops us in our tracks and in moments of sheer honesty it cuts between the facade of our social media profiles and the aspirations that escape us. We ache for recovery. We hurt for healing. We strive for true significance and purpose.

Can you identify with the crippled man in today's story? Have you been carried out to the center of town where your flaws and scars can be seen? Have you been relegated to begging those around you for a pittance of sympathy or kindness?

In the text, the crippled man, *"fixed his attention on them, expecting to receive something from them."* (Acts 3:5) The crippled man thought they would give him a few coins to sustain him for another day. Then God showed up and decided to do something special in his life, thereby sustaining him for eternity.

You can chase the acceptance of those around you, look toward the crowd for comfort, and rely on the praise of others, but in the end all anybody can give you is the best version of their own brokenness. What you really need in your deepest hurts is the healing power of the Savior. We desperately need Jesus.

But does Jesus even care about what you're going through? Does the realism of your hurt get God's attention? Of the 36 specific instances of Jesus healing or delivering an individual or group of people, over 90% of the interactions were unplanned. In the New Testament, we read[37]...

- *"At sunset, the people brought to Jesus all who had various kinds of sickness, and laying His hands on each one, He healed them." (Luke 4:40)*

- *"Jesus withdrew with His disciples to the lake, and a large crowd from Galilee followed." (Mark 3:7)*

- *"Great crowds came to Him, bringing the lame, the blind, the crippled, the mute and many others, and laid them at His feet; and He healed them." (Matt 15:30)*

- *"When Jesus had finished saying these things, He left Galilee and went into the region of Judea to the other side of the Jordan. Large crowds followed Him, and He healed them there." (Matthew 19:1–2)*

- *"Some men came carrying a paralyzed man on a mat and tried to take him into the house to lay him before Jesus." (Luke 5:18)*

- *"When He arrived at the other side." (Matthew 8:28)*

- *"A Canaanite woman from that vicinity came to Him." (Matthew 15:22)*

- *"Just then a woman who had been subject to bleeding for twelve years came up behind Him and touched the edge of His cloak." (Matthew 9:20)*

- *"When Jesus went to eat in the house of a prominent Pharisee." ((Luke 14:1)*

- *"Once more He visited Cana in Galilee." (John 4:46)*

- *"Some time later, Jesus went up to Jerusalem." (John 15:1)*

- *"They came to Bethsaida." (Mark 8:22)*

- *"Then they came to Jericho." (Mark 10:46)*

- *"As Jesus and His disciples were leaving Jericho." (Matthew 20:29)*

- *"When Jesus had entered Capernaum." (Matthew 8:5)*

- *"As Jesus went on." (Matthew 9:27)*

- *"As He went along." (John 9:1-7)*

These passages teach us Jesus isn't bothered by interruptions. Because Jesus tells us *"Come to me, all of you who are weary and carry heavy burdens, and I will give you rest."* (Matthew 11:28)

Even in the Old Testament we read, *"For I have given rest to the weary and joy to the sorrowing."* (Jeremiah 31:25)

And from the man who God used to heal the crippled man in our story, Peter encourages us to, *"Cast all your anxiety on Him because He cares for you."* (1 Peter 5:7 NIV)

One of the key lessons we uncover from Jesus' healing ministry is His unwavering focus on people. He didn't simply arrive to affect humanity in general; rather, He exhibited genuine concern and tenderness toward individuals in need of help.

Without a doubt the Bible teaches us that Jesus not only cares for you, but can also relate to you as well. The suffering He bore upon the cross, including His way to the cross, uniquely qualifies Him to connect to your sufferings. You have a Savior who understands.

The Reality of Divine Healing and the Realism of our Hurts bring us to our final discovery in this story…

THE REASON FOR GOD'S ACTIONS

"Through faith in the name of Jesus, this man was healed— and you know how crippled he was before. Faith in Jesus' name has healed him before your very eyes." (Acts 3:16)

It wasn't a particularly cold winter in January of 1983, at least not on the outside, but in the heart of a 15-year-old teen, a coldness toward God had descended upon my heart. I wasn't a candidate for divine healing, but God had other plans. A day before my family was set to move from Chicago to Phoenix I went skiing with some friends. On the way down the hill, I wiped out and injured my ankle. I was in excruciating pain, but with the coldness of the air and immediate medical attention, the swelling and pain were manageable.

The next day as we loaded the car and set our sights on a new home, my mom arranged for a man from our church to pray for me and my ankle. I wasn't thrilled about the idea since my connection with God was not a top priority at the time. In fact, I didn't even close my eyes as he prayed. But Jim Turner wasn't shy and wasn't thrown off by my snarky teen attitude. He bent down, asked if he could remove my boot, and then laid hands upon my ankle and prayed.

When he was finished, he asked how I felt. I told him I was fine, but what I didn't tell him was the heat I felt as he prayed. I put my boot back on and off we went. It was a great trip; we went from the snow to the sun in a matter of days. And in no time my ankle was back to normal. In fact, within three weeks I was climbing and descending the new mountains I discovered in

Arizona. It was quite amazing.

Five months later, in June 1983, while playing soccer I was kicked in the same ankle, and it swelled up like a balloon. I went to the hospital, and they x-rayed it. The doctor asked, "When did you break your ankle?" I said, "I didn't." He said, "Well this is a rebreak from a previous break from not too long ago." He then showed me the x-ray and I was astonished. Right before my eyes, I could see the rebreak of my ankle from five months earlier. The doctor asked me, "Who set the ankle last time because he did a pretty good job." I said, "No one, I didn't go to a doctor, but some guy from church prayed for me." I'll never forget what the doctor said: "Well I guess you could say it's a miracle because your ankle set itself perfectly five months ago."

God got my attention that day and taught me something about His divine prerogative to do whatever He wants to do, whenever He wants to do it. The doctor then smiled and asked if I wanted to call the guy from church again, or did I want him to put a cast on it this time. I opted for the cast. In fact, it was such a difficult break they eventually put a screw in my ankle to hold the bones in place during this second healing process.

I tell you that story to share with you that God still heals. This isn't just a theological topic for me, it's also a personal topic. I've experienced it. But to be clear, over the course of my life God has chosen not to show me or my family a similar type of grace in other situations.

So why does God heal? Whether it's a biblical story or a modern-day story, if God chooses to physically heal someone, He does it to reveal Himself to that person and/or to authenticate the performer of the miracle.

The New Testament teaches us this principle regarding Jesus, *"Men of Israel, listen to this: Jesus of Nazareth was a man accredited by God to you by miracles, wonders and signs, which God did among you through Him, as you yourselves know."* (Acts 2:22)

We learn a similar thing about the early apostles. *"The things that mark an apostle—signs, wonders and miracles—were done among you with great perseverance."* (2 Corinthians 12:12)

And finally, even the Gospel message was verified by God's power. *"God also testified to it by signs, wonders and various miracles, and gifts of the Holy Spirit distributed according to His will."* (Hebrews 2:4)

It's important to remember that throughout the biblical narrative, God performed numerous miracles, but it didn't necessarily cause people to believe or obey. Additionally, for any person physically healed by God, even those who were risen from the dead, eventually, another sickness or natural cause ended their earthly life. So physical healing isn't an end in itself. God simply uses the miraculous as He so chooses.

I say that to remind us that although physical healings are miraculous and point people to Christ, sometimes God utilizes our sufferings and ailments to do the same thing.

The apostle Paul is a great example. In 2 Corinthians 12:7 he reminds us that God had given him a "thorn in the flesh" and although Paul prayed for the Lord to remove it, God simply told him, *"My grace is sufficient for you, for my power is made perfect in weakness."* (2 Corinthians 12:9)

In John chapter 9 we find a man who was born blind and before Jesus healed him, He told His disciples, *"This happened so that the works of God might be displayed in him."* (John 9:3 NIV)

We all have a lot to learn on this subject. Something tells me when we get to Heaven a lot of the things we are going through or have gone through will make more sense. But in the end, it's about allowing God to use our lives as He sees fit.

In other words, I trust Him in my sickness, I trust Him for my healing, and I trust Him in my health. In all circumstances, I give thanks.

One last thought on this topic. It is possible that God can utilize your life in a way you cannot imagine, even though it appears unnatural or not normal from your perspective. Consider this from Randy Alcorn's book, *Happiness*:

The American Journal of Medical Genetics documents the results of a remarkable study of a particular people group that is not generally characterized by worry: "Among those surveyed, nearly 99% ... indicated that they were happy with their lives, 97% liked who they are, and 96% liked how they look. Nearly 99% ... expressed love for their families, and 97% liked their brothers and sisters."[38]

Who are these extraordinary people? The answer: those with Down's syndrome. "A slew of recent studies has shown that people with Down's syndrome report happier lives than us 'normal' folk. Even happier than rich, good looking and intelligent people."

The real question is, are we the ones in need of healing?

In summary, we have discovered the Reality of Divine Healing, the Realism of our Hurts, and the Reason for God's Actions as three ways God utilizes healing to teach us about His nature and to help us understand our need for Him.

CONCLUSION

Throughout this book we are discovering attributes of God as they connect to our "3:16 Verse." In this chapter, we see how God's desire to heal His people reveals an attribute of goodness. God's offer to heal shows that God is Good.

When we say God is inherently good, we mean He displays His goodness through His grace, kindness, and compassion. Everything about God is good, and He always acts in a way that reflects His goodness. The more you study the Bible, the more apparent His goodness becomes.

One example of God's goodness is evident in the first chapter of Genesis when He created the world, and everything He made was deemed "very good." (Genesis 1:31)

Additionally, the Lord's goodness extends to every individual as He is compassionate and good to all those He has created. As Psalm 145:9 states, *"The Lord is good to all; He has compassion on all He has made."*

In light of this topic on healing and suffering, what I'm learning in my life is...

- In **suffering**, we see God's grace

- In **healing**, we see God's power

- Through both, we experience God's **goodness**

"No matter what happens in our lives, God never leaves us. In His goodness, He gave us the greatest gift – the gift of His only Son Jesus. He is the goodness of God in human flesh. When we look at Jesus, we see the goodness of God."[39] - Christine Batchelder

The Bible tells us that after the crippled man was healed, "*He stood and began to walk, and entered the temple with them, walking and leaping and praising God.*" (Acts 3:8)

You may be reading this and you need help from God. You may need help physically. You may need help emotionally or spiritually. Whatever your point of need is today, Jesus is your answer. I invite you to trust Him today. If you have never put your faith and trust in Jesus, today is your day to do it.

My encouragement to you is to ask Him to meet you at your point of need. And whichever way He answers keep trusting because regardless of the situation He's always working. Whether it is through your healing or through your resting upon His grace, God's goodness will sustain you through it all.

Chapter 6

The God Who Indwells You

1 Corinthians 3:16

Attribute: God is Omnipresent

The old veterans couldn't wait to come. Roads ran thick with automobiles and horse buggies. Most arrived on the nation's sprawling rails. A few walked more than 100 miles. An 85-year-old man, fearing his son would prevent him from going, crawled out a window and caught a train.

Altogether, an estimated 50,000 of the blue and gray trekked to the Great Reunion, a grand memorial at iconic Gettysburg, on that battle's 50th anniversary: July 1st to 4th, 1913.

Why did they go? According to the many politicians and generals who also came to the reunion, the reason was clear; there was an urgent need for unity. At that very moment, U.S. ground forces were in Cuba, Mexico, Nicaragua, and the Philippines. Trouble in the Balkans threatened to escalate into a much larger European crisis. Not mentioned but certainly pressing were the many bitter divisions at home. Politicians' continual fighting over women's suffrage, overseas expansion, immigration, and labor rights. In this time of peril, so said the organizers, only the finest of military heroes could save our great nation. Most old soldiers spent their time at Gettysburg seeking something else: a chance to connect and heal.

For half a century, survivors of the nation's deadliest war struggled with memories of combat, the loss of comrades to bullets and disease, recurring nightmares, and lingering visions of killing fellow humans. Just as crippling was the loneliness. As supportive as family and friends could be, veterans needed other veterans to talk to, and their numbers were dwindling. An aging James Vernon, formerly a young lad in the 18th Virginia Infantry Regiment, said of warfare, "Those who were not there can form no idea of it."[40]

We can only imagine what our heavenly reunion will be like. There will be a chance to connect, and we'll enjoy the promise that all will be healed. Family, friends, and the heroes of faith will gather for one of Heaven's finest hours. God's plan of redemption will be complete as the original created order is finally restored.

You and I are living through a grand narrative in the story of God and His creation. This temporal frame of life is only a snapshot in comparison to the full timeline of God. *"Your life is like the morning fog—it's here a little while, then it's gone."* (James 4:14) But how do we put this in a greater context?

"In the beginning, God created the heavens and the earth." (Genesis 1:1) According to the Bible, Adam and Eve were the grand finale of God's new creation. The original couple enjoyed

a beautiful, fulfilling, and transparent relationship with their Creator. This is how it was designed. They were to enjoy the presence of God with no distractions, barriers or pretense forever.

The story was broken by their desire to disobey, and the result of their disobedience cut creation off from the Creator. Adam and Eve were banned from the Garden and thereby the presence of God was cut off from them and their descendants. Evil thought it had won. Yet the love of God would never allow that to happen.

From Genesis to Revelation, the story of God and His plan of redemption is clearly seen and understood. The grand narrative is a story of returning the presence of God to His creation.

We can divide the grand story into four scenes, the Garden, the Old Testament, the New Testament, and Heaven.

In the Garden, humanity had a perfect relationship with God and His presence was whole. In the Old Testament, the presence of God was connected to the Tabernacle or Temple. God's presence with humanity was limited to a location. In some rare cases, the presence of God was given to a person for a specific time or reason, like a prophet or King. But it was limited and mobile.

In the New Testament, Jesus, as God incarnate, was with humanity again in a specific place and for a specific time. But this time people could talk with God, touch God, cry with God, or even walk away from God as in the case of Judas. God's presence was tangible and no longer limited to a physical temple. When Christ rose from the grave and ascended into Heaven, God's personal presence departed. However, Jesus provided a game-changing promise, a promise that the presence of God would be with all who believe. *"But the Helper, the Holy Spirit, whom the Father will send in my name, He will teach you all things and bring to your remembrance all that I have said to you."* (John 14:26)

The book of Acts tells the story of the ushering in of the presence of God through the Holy Spirit in the life of the believers. That is still where we are today. We are living between the pages of the ascension of Christ and our heavenly home. In this time and in this space, the Bible teaches us that all followers of Jesus can and will experience the presence of God through the Holy Spirit.

Jesus told His disciples, *"But in fact, it is best for you that I go away, because if I don't, the Advocate won't come. If I do go away, then I will send Him to you."* (John 16:7)

This sending includes His continuous presence, *"Then I will ask the Father to send you the Holy Spirit who will help you and always be with you."* (John 14:16 CEV)

In our "3:16 Verse" today we will unpack the meaning behind a simple but powerful question asked by the apostle Paul to Christians in the city of Corinth. Packed into this one simple question are three powerful truths. These truths will help you to understand three elements of God's presence that can radically change your perspective of your Christian life and experience. It will cause you to lean into the promise and presence of God like never before.

Here's Paul's question, *"Do you not know that you are God's temple and that God's Spirit dwells in you?"* (1 Corinthians 3:16)

From this simple question we first discover…

A GREAT SPIRITUAL CONFIDENCE

"Do you not know that you are God's temple and that God's Spirit dwells in you?" (1 Corinthians 3:16)

There's something to having a bit of confidence, isn't there? Norman Vincent Peale was one of the most sought-after speakers of the 20th century. Shortly before his death, he spoke for his good friend Pastor Robert Schuler in the Crystal Cathedral. Schuler began his introduction by saying: "I want to introduce you to the most dynamic person you will ever meet in your life. He is exciting, positive, and winsome. He can reach down inside of you more deeply than anyone else you have ever known before. He will give you self-confidence and courage, and a whole lot of other things you have always wanted in your life but have not had."

Peale was astonished. He had never been introduced like this before. How could he possibly respond to this introduction? As he was trying to think of some response, he heard Schuler continue: "The person of whom I am speaking, of course, is Jesus Christ. And here to tell you about Him is my good friend, Norman."

Sometimes it's easy to agree with our own press, isn't it? We like it when people say nice things about us, especially when the people we know recognize our achievements. But as true as that is for our regular life, we're not as confident when it comes to our spiritual life.

One of the more perplexing conditions I encounter is Christians who have a lack of confidence in their walk with Christ. More specifically as it relates to knowing the presence of God in their day-to-day life.

When Paul wrote his letter to the Corinthians there was a bit of unrest in the church, and he needed to help clear things up. There was a fierce debate among the church attendees as to who was responsible for their spiritual growth and introduction to the Gospel. They were taking sides like fans during a football game. They were promoting their favorite team.

We capture the issue in chapter one, *"[11]For some members of Chloe's household have told me about your quarrels, my dear brothers and sisters. [12]Some of you are saying, 'I am a follower of Paul.' Others are saying, 'I follow Apollos,' or 'I follow Peter,' or 'I follow only Christ.' [13]Has Christ been divided into factions? Was I, Paul, crucified for you? Were any of you baptized in the name of Paul? Of course not!"* (1 Corinthians 1:11-13)

A few chapters later Paul concludes, *"[5]After all, who is Apollos? Who is Paul? We are only God's servants through whom you believed the Good News. Each of us did the work the Lord gave us. [6]I planted the seed in your hearts, and Apollos watered it, but it was God who made it grow. [7]It's not important who does the planting, or who does the watering. What's important is that God makes the seed grow. [8]The one who plants and the one who waters work together with the same purpose. And both will be rewarded for their own hard work. [9]For we are both God's workers. And you are God's field. You are God's building."* (1 Corinthians 3:5-9)

Here in verse nine, we see where Paul is leading this conversation. "You are God's building," he writes. Hold on a second, Paul, this is new information. What do you mean by saying, "You are God's building?" Don't we have a Temple in Jerusalem for that purpose? At the time of Paul's writing, it was 15 years before the Temple in Jerusalem would be leveled by the Roman empire in 70 A.D. These new Christians must have been scratching their heads with Paul's illustration.

But Paul was reminding them of something critical to their faith. Paul was reminding them that Jesus promised to send the Holy Spirit to abide with them, *"By this we know that we abide in Him and He in us, because He has given us of His Spirit."* (1 John 4:13) The word "abide" is (menō) and it means "to remain," "not to depart," or "to continue to be." In other words, we don't have to go to a certain place, at a certain time, or participate in certain rituals to experience a temporary moment with God. The days of God's presence dwelling in a building are over. His Spirit is now abiding in us, residing with us, and providing us confidence in His presence.

What kind of confidence does this lead to for a follower of Jesus? It's confidence that you belong to God. You're His property. You're His structure. You're His house.

Look how the Bible explains this in another passage, *"You heard and believed the message of truth, the Good News that He has saved you. In Him you were sealed with the Holy Spirit whom He promised."* (Ephesians 1:13 GWT) Another translation says, *"You believed in Christ, and God put His stamp of ownership on you by giving you the Holy Spirit He had promised."* (GNT)

If you're a Christian, the Bible says you've been sealed or stamped by God as His property. You're His structure. In the case of this letter to the Ephesians Paul was communicating that they were God's cargo. The word Paul uses here means, "to set a mark upon by the impress of a seal or a stamp."

In those days the cities of Ephesus and Corinth were major port cities. They were cities strategically located between Rome and trade routes from the East. Cargo ships, merchants, and political leaders all came through the ports of Ephesus and Corinth on their way to Rome. When the cargo arrived and trades were made, the new owners would affix a stamp upon the new cargo so that when it arrived in Rome the owner knew it belonged to him.

That's what happens to you and me when we become Christians. God seals us with the Holy Spirit. He puts a stamp upon you on your journey home to Heaven. It lets you, the whole world, and everything in Heaven and Hell know you belong to God. And when you arrive in Heaven, the owner knows you belong to Him.

Look at this verse in Paul's second letter to the Corinthians, *"He has identified us as His own by placing the Holy Spirit in our hearts as the first installment that guarantees everything He has promised us."* (2 Corinthians 1:22) The Holy Spirit is just the deposit. He's the guarantee of what's to come. Here on earth we gain a small deposit of God's full presence. It's a hint of the totality of God's presence one day in Heaven.

When you buy a house, you put down a deposit. You deposit "earnest money" into an account that lets the owner of the home know you want to buy that house. The Holy Spirit in your life is the "first installment" of what's to come. This is what Paul is getting at with his question, "Do you not know?" He could have said, "Are you not aware?" or "Did you forget already?" or something similar.

All of this together gives you confidence in your daily walk with Christ. You belong to Him. You are His property. You're cargo on your way home! It's time for you to walk a little taller with broad shoulders and strength in your step. This world is not your home. This world is nothing more than a rugged old cargo ship going port to port, the real excitement is when you arrive at your heavenly home. God's seal upon your life provides the confidence you need to remain focused, determined, and excited about what awaits you in Heaven.

There's a second truth we learn about God's presence. We are encouraged to develop...

A GREAT SPIRITUAL DISCIPLINE

"Do you not know that you are God's temple and that God's Spirit dwells in you?" (1 Corinthians 3:16)

When we use the word discipline some people get confused about what we mean. Are we talking about being disciplined for something we've done or are we talking about creating a life of self-control to keep us in a healthy place spiritually?

You may have heard about the mother who was cooking in the kitchen preparing a special recipe for dinner. Her little boy was creating problems by running in and out of the kitchen and ignoring his mother's wishes and warnings. When he finally knocked the special dish off the table, his mother grabbed a broom and started after him. When he crawled under the house, she decided to let her husband take care of the boy. When he arrived home from work she said, "You need to do something about our son! He needs to be disciplined!" The father crawled under the house looking around, until he saw two bright eyes peering around a pillar, and heard a soft voice say, "Dad, is that you? Is mom after you too?"

Some people think God is after them to discipline them for something bad they've done. So, they hide from Him because they're afraid. In hiding, they are completely missing out on God's presence. It happened to Adam in the garden. Do you remember what Adam and Eve did immediately after they disobeyed God? They hid from God. *"⁸And they heard the sound of the LORD God walking in the garden in the cool of the day, and the man and his wife hid themselves from the presence of the LORD God among the trees of the garden. ⁹But the LORD God called to the man and said to him, 'Where are you?' ¹⁰And he said, 'I heard the sound of you in the garden, and I was afraid, because I was naked, and I hid myself.'"* (Genesis 3:8-10)

That was a sad moment in the history of humanity, and we've been hiding from God ever since. If you've been hiding from God, it's time to come out from under the house, receive forgiveness for your actions, and move forward in pursuit of more of God in your life.

Getting back to the second part of our "3:16 Verse," we find a direct statement from Paul as if it's a matter of fact, *"You are*

God's temple." What he means here is you're not just a piece of cargo sitting on the bottom of a ship waiting to arrive at the home port someday in the future. You're an active member of God's family and your life reflects Christ. You're on active duty with all the requirements and benefits of service.

"You can judge the quality of their faith from the way they behave. Discipline is an index to doctrine." Tertullian (155-220 AD)

Just like the temple in Jerusalem was built and designed to house God's presence, now that it's gone, you and I have been built and designed to house the presence of God in our lives.

Have you wanted to experience God's presence more? It starts with putting some spiritual discipline in your life.

Loose strings provide no musical notes, but when their ends are fastened, the piano, harp, or violin is born.

Free steam drives no machine, but connected and confined with a piston and turbine, it makes an engine run.

An unconstrained river drives no turbines, but if you control a river, you generate sufficient power to light a great city.

In a similar way our lives must be disciplined if we are to be of service to God and sense His presence in a powerful way.

This was one of the lessons the apostle Paul taught the Ephesians. If you want to experience more of God's presence, remember, *"do not grieve the Holy Spirit of God, by whom you were sealed for the day of redemption."* (Ephesians 4:30).

He reminded the believers in Thessalonica, "D*o not extinguish* *the Spirit."* (1 Thessalonians 5:19 BSB)

These two passages teach us that we can actually grieve or extinguish the Holy Spirit in our life. What does that mean? It means there are actions and attitudes God doesn't want to be a part of. He doesn't want to hang out there. For example, I'm a huge Chicago Bears fan, I really don't have any interest in hanging out in a Green Bay Packers fan club. I don't like it there. I don't feel welcome there.

Similarly, God is like that with some of our actions and attitudes that don't reflect His character or nature. He doesn't like participating in these actions. Let's take a quick look at the passage Paul is referring to here in Ephesians four. There are things that "grieve" or "bring sorrow" to the heart of God.

Paul writes, *"[25]So stop telling lies. Let us tell our neighbors the truth, for we are all parts of the same body. [26]And "don't sin by letting anger control you." Don't let the sun go down while you are still angry, [27]for anger gives a foothold to the devil. [28]If you are a thief, quit stealing. Instead, use your hands for good hard work, and then give generously to others in need. [29]Don't use foul or abusive language. Let everything you say be good and helpful, so that your words will be an encouragement to those who hear them. [30]And do not bring sorrow to God's Holy Spirit by the way you live. Remember, He has identified you as His own, guaranteeing that you will be saved on the day of redemption. [31]Get rid of all bitterness, rage, anger, harsh words, and slander, as well as all types of evil behavior. [32]Instead, be kind to each other, tenderhearted, forgiving one another, just as God through Christ has forgiven you."* (Ephesians 4:25-32)

This passage along with our "3:16 Passage" reminds us that we are God's temple and as His temple, we are to be set apart for His presence in our lives. On a side note, take one or two of these per week or per month. Don't try to fix everything all at once. And as you work on these things do it with the right motives. Pursue God with love, not obligation.

Pastor and author Adrian Rogers reminds us, "Discipline says, 'I need to.' Duty says, 'I ought to.' Devotion says, 'I want to.'"

There's great Spiritual Confidence, great Spiritual Discipline, and lastly...

A GREAT SPIRITUAL EXPERIENCE

"Do you not know that you are God's temple and that God's Spirit dwells in you?" (1 Corinthians 3:16)

Did you know Celtic Christians chose not the dove, but the wild goose as a symbol representing the Holy Spirit? It sounds strange to us, but it has a long tradition in Ireland.

While the Roman Church imagined the Holy Spirit in the form of a peaceful, graceful dove, the Ancient Celts understood the Holy Spirit to be like a wild goose. When you hear of the Spirit descending like a heavenly dove, you hear harps and strings softly playing and get a peaceful feeling.

The image of a wild goose descending on you is different. A wild goose is a noisy, bothersome bird. This image jars us out of complacency. It challenges us to break out of our comfort zone. When the Holy Spirit appears in scripture, He's not depicted as safe or meek. The prophets spoke boldly, Ezekiel witnessed a vision of God's Spirit reviving dry bones, and John the Baptist preached about the Holy Spirit baptizing with fire. Paul reminded Timothy that the Spirit instills power, love, and self-discipline, not fear.

Jesus referred to the Holy Spirit as the "Spirit of the Lord" in His first sermon, quoting Isaiah, and outlining His mission to bring good news to the poor, release to the captives, healing to the blind, liberation to the oppressed, and the year of God's favor.

Clearly, the biblical description of how the Holy Spirit functions in the life of one filled with His presence is a life of enthusiasm and joy. Because you are God's temple and the Holy Spirit dwells within you, your life will radiate the presence of God.

But some people ask, how come I don't seem to feel God's presence? I go about my day and my life seems to be full of everything around me. I don't sense God in any sort of particular way. Is there something wrong with me? How come I keep missing out on the presence of God in my life?

After his decision to become a Christian, a young soldier Nicholas Herman decided to devote his life to following God and learning more about Jesus. He joined a monastery and took the name, Brother Lawrence. There he spent the rest of his life working in a kitchen and repairing his brothers' sandals. But during his decades of doing seemingly menial jobs, Brother Lawrence discovered a profound truth about having a relationship with God: Experiencing His presence can—and should—happen everywhere.

Though much of his time was spent serving others, the wisdom Brother Lawrence gleaned from praying throughout each day has been inspiring Christians for more than 300 years. His letters and discussions with peers were later compiled into the now classic book *The Practice of the Presence of God.*[41]

In one of the letters he shares, "After having given myself wholly to God, I began to live as if there was none but He and I in the world."[42]

In another letter he writes, "Sometimes I considered myself before Him as a poor criminal at the feet of his judge. At other times I beheld Him in my heart as my Father, as my God. I worshipped Him the oftenest I could, keeping my mind in His holy presence and recalling it as often as I found it wandered from Him."[43]

His book is a wonderful collection of the thoughts and process of a man who walked with God and practiced the presence of God daily. For Brother Lawrence the journey of experiencing God's presence wasn't difficult, but removing the obstacles along the road of the journey was paramount to his success.

It's like that for us as well. God's presence, as a Christian is already within us. The question isn't about God's presence, the question is are we listening? Are we too full of the things of life that we leave no room to sense God? Are we too busy with the concerns of this life that we tune out the sound of God's voice? Are we too active with the entertainment of this life that we have no room in our schedule to meet with God?

These are the questions that call us back to Christ. These are the questions that pull us closer to God. These are the questions that level the field and cut through the unimportant things that take us from our true, deep-down desire to be with God.

Is God calling you on a "Wild Goose" chase for Him? How those chases look in each of our lives varies with our gifts, skills, callings, and context, but they are all equally exciting. For some, it may require moving overseas to join a mission agency in a remote African village, but for others, it may mean taking up the charge in your current neighborhood to be salt and light, or maybe it means leading a small group or even volunteering at a homeless shelter. These are the "Wild Goose" chases we should pursue, employing our gifts, serving the local church, and advancing the kingdom.[44]

The Scriptures illustrate that God leads His people on a mission by placing special burdens on their hearts. Nehemiah was not commanded by God to rebuild Jerusalem's walls but was moved by God who had "put it into his heart" to undertake the task. (Nehemiah 2:12) Likewise, when Paul visited Athens, he was stirred by the idolatry he witnessed, which prompted him to remain there and preach the gospel. (Acts 17:16) Later he recognized a divine "ambition" within him to preach Christ in places where His name had not yet been proclaimed. (Rom. 15:20)

It's been my experience that when we fill our lives with things unrelated to the kingdom of God we crowd out or displace the presence of God in our life. Yet, when we open up our life by clearing out the unrelated things then we can sense God's presence in a more powerful way.

The question for you today is what should I clear out of my life so that I can make room for more of God's presence? Is it an action, attitude, relationship, location, or something else? If so, and God is prompting you to remove it, then do it now. Don't wait. Don't delay. Don't put it off. Take care of it now.

So, today we've come to see that just one simple question provides us with three amazing truths and these truths provide followers of Christ with Great Spiritual Confidence, Great Spiritual Discipline, and a Great Spiritual Experience.

This brings us to discover how God's presence demonstrates another one of God's attributes.

CONCLUSION

This chapter's attribute: God is Omnipresent

To say that God is omnipresent is to say He is present everywhere. Although God is not totally immersed in the fabric of creation (pantheism), He is present everywhere at all times.

God's presence is continuous throughout all of creation, though it may not be revealed in the same way at the same time to people everywhere. No molecule or atomic particle is so small that God is not fully present to it, and no galaxy is so vast that God does not circumscribe it.

At times He may be actively present in a situation, while He may not reveal that He is present in another circumstance in some other area. The Bible reveals that God can be both present to a person in a manifest manner (Psalm 46:1; Isaiah 57:15) and present in every situation in all of creation at any given time. (Psalm 33:13-14)

He is present in the person of His Son, the Lord Jesus Christ (Colossians 2:19), and supernaturally present in the Body of Christ (the Church) that covers the earth and against which the gates of Hell will not prevail.[45]

The best promise of all is God's presence to bring us peace in the midst of a messed-up world. Is your world messed up today? Is your life coming apart at the seams? Is your marriage on its last leg? Are you in a situation where all hope seems gone?

The Bible promises you when you call out to God, *"Then you will experience God's peace, which exceeds anything we can understand. His peace will guard your hearts and minds as you live in Christ Jesus."* (Philippians 4:7) This is a peace that many who do not yet know Jesus are desperate to know.

But this peace that guards your heart and mind only comes when you have peace with God through salvation. The Bible teaches us a second kind of peace, *"Therefore, since we have been made right in God's sight by faith, we have peace with God because of what Jesus Christ our Lord has done for us."* (Romans 5:1)

Where can you find peace?

The image is seared in the mind. A nine year-old girl running naked down a road screaming, arms flailing, escaping a cloud of napalm.

With a click, Nick Ut gave a human face to the horror of the Vietnam War. He photographed Kim Phuc Phan Thi as she and her friends fled from a South Vietnamese bombing raid. He took her to a hospital.

Kim survived. As she tried to escape emotional and physical pain, she found that her families' Cao Dai religion failed to comfort her. The girl in the picture became an angry, resentful woman.

She studied to be a doctor, but the government forced her to tour and speak about her ordeal. One day while looking through books at Saigon's central library, she stumbled on the New Testament. After thumbing through the gospels, two things became clear: In her traditional religion, each path to salvation depended on her effort. The Jesus she read about could carry her. He too suffered and bore scars. He had overcome.

On Christmas Eve she went to church. The pastor said Christmas was not about the gifts people give, but about the gift God gave. Moved, she walked down the aisle and said a prayer. In a moment's time, she found peace that had eluded her.

The next time you think of that sad, painful image of war, you will know how the story ended.

Or how it continues.

Maybe your scars are not visible, and your fight is not seen by others. Maybe you are screaming or running… on the inside. The peace of God which transcends human understanding can reach below the scars to heal you.

If God can do it for Kim Phuc Phan Thi, He can do it for you.

Like her, you are only a prayer away from the peace that only Jesus can bring.

Chapter 7

The God Who Pardons You

2 Corinthians 3:16

Attribute: God is Merciful

Recently I entered a world of those many consider to be forsaken. Men who have been tried and found guilty. Men serving terms in excess of 15 years to life. As I walked through the gates of one of California's high-security prisons, I was immediately drawn to the sheer amount of concrete, steel, and security. The inmates were locked up behind layers of fences, towers, and interlocking doorways. Despite the correctional facility's best attempt to create regularity in the setting, an air of hopelessness and seriousness brings tremendous weight.

Yet within this thick air of isolation, I met a group of 60 men who, though convicted of earthly crimes, have received a pardon from God on the inside. It was inspiring to see and experience the deep hope and forgiveness that only Jesus can provide. In speaking with their Chaplain, I discovered that God is at work within the prison system. The Chaplain shared with me that of the 4,000 plus inmates, over 500 of them are involved with his ministry by attending at least one of the weekend services while locked up. It's truly remarkable that in a setting designed to knock you down, these men have discovered the reality of God's love for them.

I was inspired by the words of Eric, a young man eight years into a 15-year sentence. As we ate pizza, I asked him what it means to know that God has pardoned him even though his situation looks the complete opposite. He smiled and told me, "To be pardoned by God means that my sins are forgiven. When I look at the cross it reminds me that my forgiveness is between me and God no matter what I've done. Jesus paid the price and because of that I've been set free."

As we continue on "Discovering God" we bump into another fascinating "3:16 Verse" in Paul's second letter to the Christians in the city of Corinth. Around A.D. 56, during his third missionary journey, the apostle Paul wrote 2 Corinthians while in Macedonia, (just north of modern-day Greece). He received news about the state of the Corinthian church from Titus, who had recently returned from there.

This letter provides insight into Paul's ministry and teachings as well as his deep concern for the spiritual well-being of the Corinthian congregation. This letter came after his earlier letter, 1 Corinthians, and before he wrote his well-known letter to the Romans. Remarkably, 2 Corinthians was the fourth letter Paul wrote to the Corinthian church, in addition to the letters mentioned in 1 Corinthians 5:9 and 2 Corinthians 2:3–4.

This "3:16 Passage" teaches us an important part of God's character. A part of God's character and nature that Eric and 500 other men have come to discover to be true.

"But whenever someone turns to the Lord, the veil is taken away." (2 Corinthians 3:16)

This powerful verse drives us to ask three compelling questions today. Questions that will provide you with clarity, hope, and a realization that no matter what you may have done, or no matter what may have been done to you, the wall of separation between you and your spiritual, emotional, or relational freedom will come crumbling down.

I can confidently tell you this because immediately following our "3:16 Passage," the Bible clearly teaches us, *"Where the Spirit of the Lord is, there is freedom."* (2 Corinthians 3:17) God can transform you and to set you free from your past, release you from your shackles, and propel you forward into the person He's designed you to be.

First, let's start with the opening question…

WHAT KIND OF PERSON REQUIRES A PARDON?

You probably heard about the man who wrote the IRS a note: "I haven't been able to sleep because last year, when I filled out my income tax report, I deliberately misrepresented my income. I am enclosing a check for $1,500. P.S. If I still can't sleep, I will send the rest."

The obvious answer to our first question is a person who is guilty, that's who requires a pardon. On the flip side, if you haven't done anything wrong, then you're not in need of forgiveness. Our "3:16 Passage" today starts off with the premise that we all find ourselves in a situation that requires us to turn to the Lord because we're guilty. Here it is…

"But whenever someone turns to the Lord, the veil is taken away." (2 Corinthians 3:16)

If a person doesn't read the Bible much, they may wonder what is it that a person is turning from. In order to find the answer, we need to expand a bit more on this passage. The greater passage in 2 Corinthians 3 is talking about our connection to God as human beings. Paul reviews with his audience the condition or state of humanity before Jesus showed up.

In verse 7 he writes, *"The old way, with laws etched in stone, led to death, though it began with such glory that the people of Israel could not bear to look at Moses' face. For his face shone with the glory of God, even though the brightness was already fading away."* (2 Corinthians 3:7)

This story is a call back to when Moses went to Mount Sinai to meet with God. We find this historical event in great detail in the book of Exodus. Some skeptics question the validity of the biblical record, but according to a 2016 article in the Biblical Archaeology Review, "Egyptian artifacts and sites show that the Biblical text does indeed recount accurate memories from the period to which the Exodus is generally assigned."[46]

When studied, many are surprised to find that the main elements of the book of Exodus are supported by non-biblical archaeological data. For example, this period of Egypt's history shows a significant Hebrew labor force, who hastily departed during a time of turmoil under Pharaohs whose histories match the book of Exodus. Lastly, this historical exodus occurred prior to the conquest of the land of Canaan which again matches the biblical account.

Getting back to this idea of a veil. Where does it come from?

Let's take a look at the book of Exodus. *"When Moses came down Mount Sinai carrying the two stone tablets inscribed with the terms of the covenant, he wasn't aware that his face had become radiant because he had spoken to the LORD. So when Aaron and the people of Israel saw the radiance of Moses' face, they were afraid to come near him."* (Exodus 34:30).

A few moments later the Bible tells us, *"the people of Israel would see the radiant glow of (Moses) face. So he would put the veil over his face until he returned to speak with the LORD."* (Exodus 34:35)

The veil is what prevents us from seeing the fullness of God. It's what keeps us from experiencing God in the way that we all imagined it could be. Why is it there? The presence of God was so complete that the people were afraid. God's presence is like that because He is holy. He is perfect. There isn't one spot or blemish of sin with God.

We're not like that. With us, we know we're messed up. We know we make mistakes. We know we sin. So, this isn't a new issue. We're just like the people who interacted with Moses and

Paul in both biblical examples.

What the Bible is showing us in this "3:16 Passage" is that when you "turn to the Lord," the veil (or your inability to experience God) will be removed. You will be able to experience His presence in a new way. In the way designed by God from the beginning.

So, this brings us back to the original question, what kind of person needs to be pardoned?

The Bible explains that humanity has a fatal flaw. It calls this flaw sin. Sin is a word that means to "miss the mark." In the original language, the word was used by archers to describe the distance between their target and where their arrow landed. They would say, "the sin (or distance) of my arrow is 3 feet from the target."

When the Bible uses this word to describe us, it's not referring to a physical arrow, but rather the arrow of our soul. The arrow of our decisions. The arrow of our will. In other words, how closely do we hit the target of God's perfection in our personal life?

If we're all honest, we know that we miss the target all the time. We're reminded of this in Paul's letter to Rome, *"As the Scriptures say, 'No one is righteous— not even one.'"* (Romans 3:10) A few words later Paul reminds us, *"For everyone has sinned; we all fall short of God's glorious standard."* (Romans 3:23)

Because of this fatal flaw, we are cut off from God. We have a distance between us and God. Sin separates us from Him. In short, we all need to be pardoned because we have all fallen short of

God's perfection.

Imagine if someone had a record of your entire life. Imagine if they recorded every conversation, every action, every thought, all of it. And then imagine if they sat down to review it with you. How do you think you'd feel about that? Would you be mad, upset, embarrassed, disappointed, ashamed, or humiliated? It's safe to assume that none of us would want to review our entire life in that manner. It would be unbearable.

But God did that one time in the Bible. Psalm 106 reviews Israel's history of sin and unfaithfulness. It describes the anger of the Lord toward His people, and His judgments upon them. But then it concludes: *"Nevertheless, He looked upon their distress, when He heard their cry. For their sake He remembered His covenant, and relented according to the abundance of His steadfast love."* (Psalm 106:44-45)

So even though we are people who need to be pardoned because we're all guilty, the Bible teaches us that because of God's love for us, He's prepared to come to our rescue.

This brings us to our second question...

WHAT KIND OF GOD RENDERS A PARDON?

When people think about God, eternity, and Heaven they think of all kinds of things. Some of it is right, but a lot of it is way off. A bus driver and a pastor were standing in line to get into Heaven. The bus driver approached the gate and St. Peter said, "Welcome, I understand you were a bus driver. Since I'm in charge of housing, I believe I have found the perfect place for you. See that mansion over the hilltop? It's yours."

The pastor heard all this and began to stand a little taller. He said to himself, "If a bus driver got a place like that, just think what I'll get."

The pastor approached the gate and St. Peter said, "Welcome, I understand you were a minister. See that shack in the valley?"

St. Peter had hardly gotten the words out of his mouth when the irate minister said, "I was a minister, I preached the gospel, I helped teach people about God. Why does that bus driver get a mansion, and I get a shack?"

Sadly St. Peter responded, "Well, it seems when you preached, people slept. When the bus driver drove, people prayed."

If we really understood God, we would be amazed at how loving He really is toward us. We get it wrong so many times. Think about it. Jesus walked in the midst of thousands upon thousands of people during His time on earth and very few caught a glimpse of what He was all about. Even the ones He personally helped got it wrong. What this tells us is we really need to spend some time considering who God is and what kind of God renders us a pardon.

A great place to start is in the gospels. These four letters tell us all about Jesus. These letters explain who He is, what He did, and the way in which He described Himself to us.

In one of Jesus' very first stories, we find an incredible insight into what God is like. Here's what Luke records, "*14Then Jesus returned to Galilee, filled with the Holy*

Spirit's power. Reports about Him spread quickly through the whole region. [15]He taught regularly in their synagogues and was praised by everyone. [16]When He came to the village of Nazareth, His boyhood home, He went as usual to the synagogue on the Sabbath and stood up to read the Scriptures. [17]The scroll of Isaiah the prophet was handed to Him. He unrolled the scroll and found the place where this was written:

> *'[18]The Spirit of the Lord is upon me, for He has anointed me to bring Good News to the poor.*
>
> *He has sent me to proclaim that captives will be released, that the blind will see, that the oppressed will be set free, [19]and that the time of the Lord's favor has come.'*
>
> *[20]He rolled up the scroll, handed it back to the attendant, and sat down. All eyes in the synagogue looked at Him intently. [21]Then He began to speak to them. 'The Scripture you've just heard has been fulfilled this very day!'" (Luke 4:14-22)*

At that moment Jesus was telling His audience that He was the long-awaited Messiah. He's the One to deliver God's people from their sins. In the middle of this passage from Isaiah 61 we see that Jesus came to release the captives, give sight to the blind, and set free the oppressed. He did that while He was here. But it means more than just physical healings or one-time miracles for people 2,000 years ago. His work back then makes an impact today.

It means He delivers us from our spiritual blindness, oppression, and captivity. A captivity caused by our sin. An oppression driven by our selfishness. A blindness caused by our unrighteousness. Our condition of being far from God isn't caused by God, it's caused by our own actions.

But what we're learning in this passage is that God loves you so much that He doesn't want you to stay in your lost condition. He came to rescue you. He came to save you. He came to pardon you. Have you received His gift of salvation yet?

Jesus removes the veil that separates you from God. *"But whenever someone turns to the Lord, the veil is taken away."* (2 Corinthians 3:16) This is the part I'd really like to impress upon you.

In the Old Testament, and up to the time of Jesus, there was a huge veil that separated the Holy of Holies from the regular part of the Temple. This signified that man was separated from God by sin. When Jesus died upon the cross, the gospel writers record that this veil was actually ripped in two, from top to bottom, *"At that moment the veil of the temple was torn in two from top to bottom."* (Matthew 27:51 BSB) The ripping of the veil during Jesus' death was a powerful representation of His sacrifice, where He shed His blood as a complete atonement for sins. It conveyed the message that the path to the Holy of Holies was now open to everyone, regardless of whether they were Jewish or Gentile, and this availability would remain open for all time.

Additionally, this event signaled that God would no longer be present in a temple constructed by human hands. This is exactly what Paul mentions to the people of Athens, *"The God who made the world and everything in it, being Lord of heaven and earth, does not live in temples made by man."* (Acts 17:24) Everything changed the moment Christ died on the cross.

But there's a second thing I want you to see today. When our "3:16 Passage" says, "the veil is taken away," this also means your ability to receive this message and understand it. In other words, have you ever wondered why everyone doesn't understand the gospel message? Why doesn't everyone just believe?

We find a clue in chapter 4, "*it is veiled to those who are perishing.⁴In their case the god of this world has blinded the minds of the unbelievers.*" (2 Corinthians 4:3-4)

This whole message of God's love, God's forgiveness, and God's grace to you in receiving and understanding His message of mercy is only provided to us because of His compassion and love for you.

Our response to this love brings us to our third question for today…

WHAT KIND OF LIFE
REFLECTS A PARDON?

In his book *When I Relax, I feel Guilty*, Tim Hansel provides an insight into what most people want from God:

"I would like to buy $3.00 worth of God, please. Not enough to explode my soul or disturb my sleep, but just enough to equal a cup of warm milk or a snooze in the sunshine. I don't want enough of Him to make me love someone different or pick beets with a migrant. I want happiness, not transformation; I want the warmth of the womb, not a new birth. I want a pound of the

Eternal in a paper sack. I would like to buy $3.00 worth of God, please."

How many times do we limit God in our lives? We think, "I don't need to go all in for God." Or "I'll receive God's gift of salvation, but this idea of transformation, let's hold off on that." I think we resist change because it takes work, sacrifice, or commitment.

In this text Paul teaches these new Christians (in Corinth) that when you become a follower of Christ something happens to you beyond receiving a pardon for your sin. He tells them, "(God) has enabled us to be ministers of His new covenant." (2 Corinthians 3:6) This means you become a person on God's roster that is ready and able to get into the game when He calls your number.

When I was a kid, I loved playing basketball. I remember sitting on the bench all suited up and ready to go; laces tied, uniform tucked in, and paying attention to the game. Why? Because when the coach looked down the row and called my name, I knew I had to be ready. I'd jump to my feet, run over to the scorer's table and check into the game.

Paul is saying here that God has "enabled us." In the original language, this phrase means "to equip one with adequate power to perform the duties."[47] Going all in for God and getting into the game isn't something you have to muster up all on your own. You go all in for God because God has gone all in for you.

God empowers you. He's provided you with certain gifts, talents, and abilities. The key for you is finding the area of serving and sharing that fits how God designed you.

What kind of life reflects a pardon? A life that is thankful. When Christ saves you, when Jesus redeems you, when God pulls you up from out of your situation, cleanses your wrongdoings, and sets your feet on the solid ground of His Word, you can't help but rejoice and be incredibly thankful.

In John 9, the Bible tells us about a blind man Jesus healed. The religious people (the skeptics) quizzed the man to find out what happened. The man didn't know Old Testament prophecies or understand theology, but he did know that God did something special in his life. The Bible says it like this, *"The man replied. 'But I know this: I was blind, and now I can see!'"* (John 9:25)

David writes, *"He lifted me out of the pit of despair, out of the mud and the mire. He set my feet on solid ground and steadied me as I walked along. He has given me a new song to sing, a hymn of praise to our God. Many will see what He has done and be amazed. They will put their trust in the LORD."* (Psalm 40:2-3)

God wants to use your life, your testimony, and your story to encourage those in your world with the good news of God's love. The question for you is will you open your life to others in a way that allows God to use you to share His love?

Conclusion

This chapter's attribute: God is Merciful

When we say God shows us mercy, we're saying that God doesn't give us what we deserve. That's what mercy is. It's not getting what you deserve.

Grace is getting what you don't deserve.

Mercy is not getting what you do deserve.

We deserve judgment. We deserve to be cut off from God forever. We deserve a verdict of guilty. But God doesn't do that. Because of the cross, Jesus took all of that upon Himself. He bore our sin. He carried our sentence. He paid a debt He did not owe. We owed a debt we could not pay.

When we "Turn to the Lord" as the "3:16 Passage" tells us, the veil is removed because of God's mercy. He brings us into right fellowship with Him even though we don't deserve it.

You may be reading this and you need God's mercy because you've never given your life over to Jesus. You've tried living life your way, but you've found it empty.

There's a hole in the center of your heart and you've tried filling it with everything you can imagine: people, substances, media, entertainment, self-centeredness, but none of it works. You're cut off from God and you need His mercy today, and you can sense it deep in your soul.

Karel Versteeg was in the Dutch resistance in World War II. Arrested in 1942, he was to be executed immediately. Instead, he was handed over to a German officer.

Versteeg said to the German officer, "Listen, If you were in the same situation I am in, if your country had just been occupied by another country, if your city was Rotterdam and was on fire and had been leveled to the ground, what would you do?" The officer replied: "I would do the exact same thing you are doing. I would fight back." So, he showed mercy and put him in solitary confinement for two years.

After the war, the German officer who spared Karel Versteeg's life was on trial for his own life. Versteeg went to Nuremberg, told the story, and testified on behalf of his enemy, showing mercy, thereby saving his enemy's life.

In 2013, Karel's grandson, Canadian singer, Menno Versteeg, wrote a song about his grandfather's story called "So It Goes."

The most remarkable part of the story is what happened after the video was released. With the help of the Dutch government, Versteeg was able to track down the grandson of the German soldier who saved his grandfather's life. The two grandchildren spoke on the phone, met in person, and bonded over their shared connection to this incredible story of mercy.

Versteeg said, "Although he's a person on the other side of the world, our lives are intertwined in such an interesting way. And if our grandparents hadn't met during such an awful time and had the opportunity to speak with each other and develop mutual respect, neither I nor the grandson of the German officer would be alive today."

When we show mercy, we stop the cycle of separation and destruction. We end the wars of bitterness and resentment in our life. Because these two men chose mercy over justice their story, and their families, continue today.

The same is true for you in your relationship with God. God has chosen to show you mercy. He's ready to give you a pardon. He has provided a way for you to receive forgiveness and grace. He wants your story to continue. Not only here... but also with Him for all eternity.

Would you like to receive God's forgiveness today and begin living life under His mercy?

You can have it today.

Chapter 8

The God Who Calms You

2 Thessalonians 3:16

Attribute: God is Faithful

Have you noticed how forgetting something can turn a peaceful and calm situation into a quick moment of panic? I was having a great morning thinking about all God is going to do one Sunday at Compass Church and the lives that would be changed. Then I realized I forgot to charge my phone last night…and what started out as a calm, peaceful day all of a sudden turned into a bunch of stress.

This reminds me of the couple in their nineties who were both having problems remembering. During a checkup the doctor told them that they're physically okay, but they might want to start writing things down to help them remember.

Later that night, while watching TV, the old man got up from his chair:

Husband: "Want anything while I'm in the kitchen?" he asked.

Wife: "Will you get me a bowl of ice cream?"

Husband: "Sure."

Wife: "Don't you think you should write it down so you can remember it?" She asked.

Husband: "No, I can remember it."

Wife: "Well, I'd like some strawberries on top, too. Maybe you should write it down, so you don't forget it?"

Husband: Said, "I can remember that. You want a bowl of ice cream with strawberries."

Wife: "I'd also like whipped cream. I'm certain you'll forget that. Write it down," she said.

Husband: Irritated, he said, "I don't need to write it down, I can remember it! Ice cream with strawberries and whipped cream - I got it, for goodness' sake!"

Then he walked into the kitchen. After about 20 minutes, the old man returned and hands his wife a plate of bacon and eggs. She stares at the plate for a moment.

Wife: "Where's my toast?"

In a world that can be chaotic and overwhelming, we know there is a source of peace and comfort that can help us find our way. It's found in our next "3:16 Verse."

Here's what it says, *"Now may the Lord of peace Himself give you peace at all times and in every way."*

This verse promises us that we are not alone in our struggles. God can bring us peace and calm even in the midst of chaos.

Whether you are dealing with stress at work, tension in your relationships, or simply feeling overwhelmed by the demands of daily life, Jesus offers you peace and security when life brings chaos and confusion.

In this chapter I want to talk to you about three elements of peace and because we serve a God who is faithful, He can bring incredible calm to your life.

Let's first look at...

THE PERSON OF PEACE

"Now may the Lord of peace Himself give you peace at all times and in every way." (2 Thessalonians 3:16)

As we begin our journey through this short passage, we can't help but notice the first reference to Jesus in the first six words. Some skeptics or doubters of Jesus may question the uniqueness of Jesus and His overall impact upon our world, but according to history, Jesus has made quite an impact.

Socrates taught for 40 years, Plato for 50, Aristotle for 40, and Jesus for only 3. Yet the influence of Christ's 3-year ministry outlasts the impact of the combined 130 years of teaching from these men, some of the greatest philosophers of history.

Consider this...

Jesus painted no pictures yet some of the finest paintings of Michelangelo and Leonardo da Vinci received their inspiration from Him.

Jesus wrote no poetry, but Dante, Milton, and scores of the world's greatest poets were inspired by Him.

Jesus built no buildings, but St. Peter's Cathedral in Rome and Notre Dame in Paris are some of the most beautiful buildings in the world.

Jesus composed no music yet Handel, Beethoven, and Bach, reached their highest perfection of melody in the hymns and symphonies they composed for His praise.

Every sphere of human greatness has been enriched by this humble Carpenter of Nazareth.

His unique contribution to humanity is the salvation of the soul!

Philosophy could not accomplish that. Nor art. Nor literature. Nor music.

Only Jesus Christ can break the enslaving chains of sin. He alone can speak peace to the human heart, strengthen the weak, and give life to those who are spiritually dead.

Jesus is the person of peace!

We are learning just how much anxiety plagues our culture. But what does anxiety mean and how much of an impact on our culture are we really experiencing? According to a recent *Psychology Today* article, "Anxiety is both a mental and physical state of negative expectation. It is characterized by increased apprehension leading to worry." The article continues, "Anxiety is now the leading mental health problem around the world, and the incidence of anxiety is still rising."[48]

Many factors contribute to the root cause of anxiety and in some cases, proper medical care is very important and a positive avenue to pursue. But in many cases the root cause of our anxiety, worry, fear, and tension is based on not having solid foundational truth in our life. It's as though many of our "foundations of life" have been built on shifting sand.

The Bible teaches us that Jesus is truth. He's a solid foundation. Through Him, you and I can have ultimate peace, not only because He's a solid foundation, but also because He is peace.

You most likely noticed, the Scripture refers to Jesus as, "the Lord of peace." This is an important part of New Testament thinking. Long before this letter from Paul to the Thessalonians, New Testament readers already attributed peace as coming from God. But since the time of Jesus, the idea of finding real peace was being attached to Jesus in a personal way.

In the Old Testament, the Angel of the LORD represented God's physical presence on earth. Theologians call this a theophany. It's when the presence of God takes on a physical form in the Old Testament. We have an example of this in Judges 6.

In the story, Gideon had a life-changing encounter with the Angel of the LORD. God charged Gideon with the seemingly impossible task of defeating the Midianites. Gideon became fearful for his life.

However, the Lord reassured him, saying, *"Peace be to you. Do not fear; you shall not die."* (Judges 6:23) In response, Gideon built an altar of worship and named it "The LORD is Peace." (Judges 6:24)

143

In Hebrew this is pronounced Jehovah Shalom. This is the only time in the Bible the phrase is used. This event emphasizes the notion that peace is not just a concept, but a person – the Lord Himself. When Jesus is referred to as "the Lord of peace" these New Testament readers knew exactly what Paul was saying about Jesus.

In the New Testament peace followed Jesus wherever He went. Fear, sickness, pain, and disease vanished at His touch. Through the power of His spoken word, He restored mental and emotional health, and brought about physiological peace.

His jurisdiction of influence extended beyond people's lives, as shown in Mark 4 when a great windstorm arose while the disciples were on the sea of Galilee. Despite the chaos around Him Jesus was able to sleep in the boat because of the peace He carried within. The disciples, on the other hand, (just like Gideon) were afraid for their lives and woke Him up. Jesus responded by commanding the storm to be still, *"Peace! Be still!"* (Mark 4:39)

The peace that He had within Himself created an instant calm in His environment. He was able to create peace because He embodied peace itself.

Jesus is often associated with peace in the Bible. In fact, He is referred to as the "Prince of Peace" in the book of Isaiah (Isaiah 9:6). Throughout the New Testament, Jesus talks about peace and how it should be a central focus for His followers.

In the Sermon on the Mount, Jesus says, *"Blessed are the peacemakers, for they will be called children of God."* (Matthew 5:9 NIV)

In John 14:27, Jesus tells His disciples, *"Peace I leave with you; my peace I give you. I do not give to you as the world gives. Do not let your hearts be troubled and do not be afraid."* (NIV)

In Matthew 11:28-30, Jesus invites all who are weary and burdened to come to Him and find rest. He promises that His yoke is easy, and His burden is light, bringing peace to those who follow Him.

In John 16:33, Jesus tells His disciples, *"In this world you will have trouble. But take heart! I have overcome the world."* (NIV) Jesus acknowledges the difficulties of life, but also promises peace through faith in Him.

In Ephesians 2:14, the apostle Paul writes, *"For He Himself is our peace, who has made the two groups one and has destroyed the barrier, the dividing wall of hostility."* (NIV)

In Colossians 3:15, Paul encourages believers to let the peace of Christ rule in their hearts and to be thankful.

I like how author Don Everts summarizes the life of Jesus:

"Jesus was entirely different and new and stunning. There was just something so clear and beautiful and true and unique and powerful about Jesus that old rabbis would marvel at His teaching, young children would run and sit in His lap, ashamed prostitutes would find themselves weeping at His feet, whole villages would gather to hear Him speak, experts in the law would find themselves speechless, and people from the poor to the rugged working class to the unbelievably wealthy would leave everything ... to follow him."[49]

Do you want to know why Jesus was so popular back then and

why He's still so popular today? Because, when you get close to Jesus, you experience true peace.

Next let's look at…

THE PROCESS OF PEACE

"Now may the Lord of peace Himself give you peace at all times and in every way." (2 Thessalonians 3:16)

In Valyermo, California, (about an hour north of LA) a group of monks converted a 400-acre ranch into a religious community called St. Andrew's Abbey. As you enter the grounds, there's a captivating sign for all to see: "No Hunting Except for Peace."

People are hunting for all sorts of things, aren't they? They're hunting for significance, entertainment, relationship, well-being, variety, money, and success. But how about you? What are you hunting for? Are you hunting for peace?

The monks at St. Andrews are on to something. They've found the benefit of looking at life through the long lens of eternity instead of the short lens of the temporary.

So many times we look for a substitute, a small measure of peace. Just enough peace to get you through the current crisis or situation. But when you understand biblical peace, it'll take you much higher, much deeper, and much wider.

If peace really is a person, and the person is Jesus, then the monks of St. Andrew got it right because Jesus is eternal. And when you get Jesus, you get peace…the hunt for peace is over.

The Bible reminds us, Far better to take refuge in God than trust in people; Far better to take refuge in God than trust in celebrities. (Psalm 118:8-9 MSG) This word refuge (חָסָה ḥāsâ) in the original language means "to flee for protection, to confide in—have hope, (put) trust."

Who do you flee to when you're in trouble? Who do you go to when you're in turmoil? Where do you turn to when you're pressed in on all sides and you can't find a way out? What's your last resort plan?

Let's climb back into our "3:16 Passage." Paul wrote this small letter, II Thessalonians, to Christians in the city of Thessalonica. This was another port city important to that region of the world. It was in modern-day Greece tucked away in a northern bay of the Aegean Sea. It was settled along a famous road, the Via Egnatia. An ancient highway constructed by the Romans in the 2nd century BC that stretched from Rome to Istanbul.

Paul visited Thessalonica in 51 AD, only 18 years after the resurrection of Jesus. His visit and ministry are captured for us in Acts 17. The Bible says a mob formed because Paul's ministry was so effective. His message was effective because his message of peace brought true peace to the common people of the city. But jealousy set in and some city leaders complained, *"These men who have turned the world upside down have come here also...they are all acting against the decrees of Caesar, saying that there is another king, Jesus."* (Acts 17:6-7) Paul and Silas left the city to avoid a riot and ended up in Berea.

A few months later, while in the city of Corinth, Paul decided to check up on the new believers in Thessalonica, so he sent

Timothy back to the city. Timothy returned with a positive report but with some major questions from the people. (1 Thessalonians 3:1-7)

The majority of Paul's two letters to the Thessalonians deal with questions the new followers of Jesus had. They had questions about the end times, the return of Jesus, and what happens to us when we die. Theologians recognize these two letters as eschatological (end times) letters. Most agree these two letters from Paul cover the subject in far greater detail than in any of Paul's other letters.

The overall frustration, fear, tension, and anxiety felt by these early Christians shouldn't be overlooked. They were surrounded by negative people in a hostile religious and political environment. They were working with, doing business with, interacting, and engaging with a culture that was very hostile and unfriendly to their faith.

Yet within this environment Paul writes, *"Now may our Lord Jesus Christ Himself, and God our Father, who loved us and gave us eternal comfort and good hope through grace, 17comfort your hearts and establish them in every good work and word."* (2 Thessalonians 2:16-17) The prayer of Paul is for comfort to reign over anxiety, for peace to rule over worry, and for confidence to reign over fear.

How does God provide His peace for you? What is God's process for peace? Just like there's a process of making bread or forming pottery, there's a process of understanding how God provides peace through Christ.

We can break it down into three practical steps:

1. REALIZE THE GIFT

Jesus knew that His followers, both present and future, would face challenges and dangers in their ministry and life, but He didn't want them (or us) to live in fear. He reminded His disciples, *"I am leaving you with a gift—peace of mind and heart. And the peace I give is a gift the world cannot give. So don't be troubled or afraid."* (John 14:27) This means you don't have to create, invent, generate, or design peace. It's something given to you by God. Since Jesus is peace, it all flows from Him. Go after Jesus and you get peace.

2. RECOGNIZE HIS WORD

There is incredible power in the Word of God. Never underestimate the power of the written Word. When Jesus did battle with the devil, He did so by quoting Scripture. The devil quoted Scripture too, but if you look closely, the devil misquoted it, manipulated it, or misrepresented it. But Jesus wasn't fazed by the devil's misdeeds. Jesus kept His heart and mind steadied on the Word of God. He spoke it, rested on it, and stayed on it. He was unwavering, unmoved, and unaffected by the plans of the enemy. He reminded His disciples that God uses His Work, once spoken, now written, so that we may have peace in His word(s). Here's what Jesus said, *"These things I have spoken to you, so that in Me you may have peace. In the world you have tribulation but take courage; I have overcome the world."* (John 16:33 NASB)

3. REORGANIZE YOUR WORRIES

In His presence, we have the power to overcome the stress of the present or the anxiety of the future. The Bible says, you are to

"Give all your worries and cares to God, for He cares about you."
(1 Peter 5:7) You need to stop transporting your worries. Quit giving your worries a free ride. Hand them over to someone who can handle them. Some people think they can't hand over their worries and cares to God because He's too busy taking care of all the affairs of the universe. It is true that God looks after the entirety of His creation, but never think for a minute that He doesn't care for you or doesn't have the capability to do so.

There is an intriguing bit of Scripture in Revelation 1:16-18. John a lonely prisoner on the barren cliffs of the island of Patmos, writes that he saw the glorified Christ, the one "who lives and was dead," who is "alive forevermore."

During this vision, John writes, "(Jesus) had in His right hand seven stars," and upon seeing Jesus, "I fell down at His feet as one dead." Then, the very next word is this: "He laid His right hand on me."

His right hand? Do you mean the hand with the seven stars in it? Yes, that hand.

What about the seven stars? Jesus must have laid them aside somewhere. It must be an important task to hold seven stars in one's hand. But to hold these is not more important to Jesus than to touch a person who is bowed before Him in worship.

This is the kind of God we worship – a God who puts aside the care of stars to care for one person who comes in reverence to Him. Know this: whatever else in the whole universe may be of concern to Jesus right now, nothing is more important to Him than you are. As you humbly bring your concerns to Him, His hand of peace is resting upon your shoulder.

We've seen the person of peace and the process of peace, finally, let's look at…

THE PROMISE OF PEACE

"Now may the Lord of peace Himself give you peace at all times and in every way." (2 Thessalonians 3:16)

Much of our life is about restrictions, boundaries, and limits. We have speed limits on our roads. We have boundaries on our property. And we have restrictions on our diets. For the most part, these types of limitations are healthy and needed. They provide safety, protection, and clarity.

But when it comes to God and His promise of peace, we see the lid of limitation blown off its hinge. According to our "3:16 Passage," there are no limits to God's peace. Paul writes you can experience God's peace, "at all times and in every way."

On a personal level, I find this final portion of the passage to be extremely interesting. That's not to limit or disregard the prior two sections of the verse. But I'm more familiar and comfortable with the idea of Jesus being the embodiment of peace because that makes sense to me on an ontological level. And that He provides His people with peace aligns with common sense logic to me. But this idea of always having peace in every way appears to be a bit more perplexing to me.

If we take the passage at face value, it means that in every situation I can experience God's peace. So does it mean I can experience the peace of God when I stub my toe? How about when

I lose my job? Or, when my kid goes off the rails? When my spouse tells me, "It's over!"? When the Dr. says I should get my affairs in order? When my entire savings and retirement has been swindled or lost?

Some of you may be going through one of these situations right now and you're wondering, "How in the world can I find the peace of God in the middle of this confusion and pain?"

Let me take you back to the Thessalonians for a minute. When Paul wrote his second letter, it was most likely only six months after the first letter. The purpose of the two back-to-back letters was driven by the fact that these new Christians were very troubled. They loved Jesus. They were following His teachings. They were doing everything right in honoring God with their lives and in their businesses. They weren't perfect, but they were heading in the right direction.

But they were under tough persecution. They were in a heated political climate. They endured a never-ending stream of false teachers. And because of that, they developed a strong fear of the future that they had actually missed the return of Jesus. They were scared, petrified, worried, and frightened. These were real concerns, real hurts, real fears, and real sufferings.

Under the influence and direction of the Holy Spirit, Paul led these young Christians into an amazing truth. A truth that you can lean on today as well. Here it is: The promises of God are stronger than anything you will face on this planet. The promises of God are tougher than anything you will encounter in this life. The promises of God are more resilient than anything you will confront in this world.

He focuses their attention not on their situation, but on their salvation. Not on their problem, but on God's promises. Not on their hardship, but in their final healing at the return of Jesus.

Nearly 40 percent of Paul's second letter deals with the second coming of Christ. When you focus your attention on God's promises and ultimate redemption it helps to refocus your hurts and move you forward in a way that has a strong foundation.

One thing I've learned in life is that I cannot control what happens around me, or sometimes to me, but I can control what happens inside of me. I'm the only one who gets to decide what I think about, what I focus on, what I dwell on, what I tell myself, what I consider and how I consider it, and to what level.

What I can strongly say is, if you are full of the promises of God, when you go internal, when you go deep inside, you'll find a reservoir so full of the Truth of God's Word that you can't help but find peace. But if you're empty inside and all you have is platitudes, worldly ideologies, empty slogans, or false promises from those who are just as lost as you are, when you go deep into that, that's when you find true emptiness.

Here's a list of God's Promises:

- An acceptance that can never be questioned. (Ephesians 1:6)

- An inheritance that can never be lost. (I Peter 1:3-5)

- A deliverance that can never be excelled. (2 Corinthians 1:10)

- A grace that can never be limited. (2 Corinthians 12:9)

- A hope that can never be disappointed. (Hebrews 6:18, 19)

- A bounty that can never be withdrawn. (I Colossians 3:21-23)

- A joy that need never be diminished. (John 15:11)

- A nearness to God that can never be reversed. (Ephesians 2:13)

- A peace that can never be disturbed. (John 14:27)

- A righteousness that can never be tarnished. (2 Corinthians 5:21)

- A salvation that can never be canceled. (Hebrews 5:9)[50]

How do I get this? How can I lay hold of these Godly promises?

John Paton was a missionary to the South Pacific. He soon discovered that while the native people had words for house, tree, and stone, they had no words for love, joy, and peace. Worst of all, they had no word for believe. One day as he sat in his hut filled with frustration, an old indigenous man entered and slumped down in a chair. Exhausted from a long journey, the man said, "I'm leaning my whole weight on this chair." "What did you say?" asked Paton. The man repeated, "I'm leaning my whole weight on this chair." Immediately, Paton shouted, "That's it!" And from that day forward for that primitive tribe, "Believe in Jesus" became "Lean your whole weight on Jesus."

Have you leaned your entire weight on Jesus yet?

The Person, Process, and Promise of peace teach us another part of God's nature. He is a God that is faithful.

CONCLUSION

This chapter's attribute: God is Faithful

The Bible frequently mentions God's faithfulness, emphasizing that He always follows through on His promises, regardless of how impossible those promises may seem. This has been true throughout history, remains true in the present, and will continue to be true in the future.

God's faithfulness is a fundamental attribute of His character, and if He were to be unfaithful even once, He would cease to be God and we could not trust in any of His promises.

However, as it is written, *"Not one word has failed of all the good promises He gave."* (1 Kings 8:56 NIV) God's faithfulness is an essential and unchanging aspect of His nature. (Psalm 89:8) The Bible reminds us, *"Jesus Christ is the same yesterday, today, and forever."* (Hebrews 13:8) Faithfulness is not something God has to strive for or work at; He is inherently faithful, eternally steadfast, and unwavering.

His faithfulness is rooted in His sovereignty, which means God is in control, therefore I can relax. He's got this!

Calm, a sleep and meditation app, had sales of $200 million in 2020, a 33% increase in one year. Anxiety symptoms increased from 8.1% in 2019 to 25.5% in 2020. Thirty-one percent of college students have an anxiety disorder. Over forty-one percent of 18-29-year-olds suffer from anxiety. Apps and techniques, helpful as they are, don't calm our fear of death or loss when the earth shakes.

On February 6th, an earthquake struck southern and central Turkey, and northern and western Syria. More quakes followed. Over 59,000 people died. Rabbi Abraham Cooper was speaking to a friend who lost 23 family members. "Then, according to Cooper, she said something that shocked us."

She said: "There is some good news I wanted you to know... the church survived, and so did the Torah scrolls – someone saved them from the destroyed synagogue." She wanted to make sure we knew – as Christians and Jews — with nearly everything destroyed, God left us – the children of Abraham — the promises of His Word.

The disciples cried for help in a storm and Jesus calmed the sea, but their questions were personal: "God, where are you" and "Do you even care?" Elijah was in a windstorm, an earthquake, and a fire. God showed up in a whisper.

God encourages us to calm down by looking up, to get close, and realize that when everything is moving, we need to reach for that which can't be moved.

Jesus is your peace during the storm. God calms your fears by being present.

Have you invited Jesus to be with you in the middle of what you're going through? He cares for you, He really does. He's here for you today not only to be with you but to provide you with peace that will calm you.

Chapter 9

The God Who Guides You

2 Timothy 3:16

Attribute: God is All-Knowing

Have you ever been lost? In a world before iPhones and Google maps, it was a bit more common to get lost. One of the several jobs that helped get me through college was to work for Domino's Pizza in downtown Minneapolis. Not only could I spin up a pepperoni pizza and get it in the oven in less than 30 seconds, but I could also get that pizza to your front door in under 30 minutes. Some of you may recall Domino's fast-delivery promise to deliver your pizza in 30 minutes or less or it's free. Sounds a bit cavalier for today, but things were different in the 1980s.

Now when you're a college student new to town and there's zero technology to provide direction while you drive, you quickly learn the store map is your guidance system. I remember for the first three or four months staring at the huge map attempting to memorize the street names, one-way roads, freeways, and quickest routes. Because once in the car, there was no time to pull over and review an old-school fold-out map. That was for backup purposes only. It had to be an emergency.

In those early days I got lost a few times, but for the most part I was able to get my bearings and get back on track to the destination. But over time as I became more and more familiar with the map and committed its content to memory it was like I had an internal guidance system built inside of me. I knew the city of Minneapolis like the back of my hand. Every alley, every bridge, every construction zone, and loading zone, was all memorized. I even had all the green lights timed to perfection based on which direction I was headed. It is amazing how precisely unlost you can feel when you focus your attention on gaining proper guidance.

Life is like that, isn't it? It's about gaining proper guidance. The question becomes which map are you memorizing. Because the map in your head will determine the direction you'll be going. Life is full of questions and uncertainties. We all face moments when we don't know which way to turn. I've learned that life is dependent on how well you get proper guidance. Especially when it comes to your spiritual life because it's essential to end up where God wants you to go. If you have the wrong map, you'll end up in a spiritually dark alleyway lost and confused wondering how you got there. Dazed, lost, and confused.

So to help you, I want to share a source of truth and wisdom that can help you find your way. To help you find the right way, the right path, the right map. 2 Timothy 3:16 begins, *"All*

Scripture is inspired by God and is useful for teaching the truth, rebuking error, correcting faults, and giving instruction for right living, so that the person who serves God may be fully qualified and equipped to do every kind of good deed."

The Bible is more than just a collection of stories. It is a powerful tool for your growth and transformation. Through its pages, you can learn valuable lessons about yourself, your world, and your relationship with God.

Whether you are seeking answers to life's big questions, struggling with personal challenges, or simply looking for inspiration and guidance, 2 Timothy 3:16 tells us that the Bible can offer you the wisdom and insight you need.

So why not open yourself up to the power of Scripture today, and let it transform your life? With an open heart and a willingness to learn, you can discover the beauty and richness of God's Word. I'd like to uncover for you three distinctions about God's Word as found in our next "3:16 Passage" today.

First let's look at…

THE DESCRIPTION OF GOD'S WORD

"All Scripture is inspired by God and is useful for teaching the truth, rebuking error, correcting faults, and giving instruction for right living, so that the person who serves God may be fully qualified and equipped to do every kind of good deed." (2 Timothy 3:16,17 GNT)

The passage begins by declaring that the Bible is inspired by

God. Not just some of it or part of it, but all of it. This first point is dealing with the question, How do you know which map is the right map? When I walked into that Domino's Pizza for the first time, I didn't really question if the huge map on the wall was accurate because all the other drivers were using it, and nobody brought up any issues with it. In other words, it worked. I tried it and it proved to be true. It was accurate. It matched the outside world when I left the store. It was true to reality.

That's one of the ways you can test a map to see if it's accurate. Does it match reality? Does it connect or relate to my experiences? Billions of people have tried and tested the Bible over the past 3,400 years and it has been found to be accurate to the real world. The Bible remarkably describes our human condition and connects to our deepest needs. But beyond this, and far more important is its quality of divine inspiration.

What does it mean to say the Bible is Inspired by God?

One translation (ESV) says the word for "inspired" is translated as "to be breathed out by God." That's a very good translation because in the original language, the two words used for this phrase were theos and pneo. That means God and wind. So, the Greek word, (θεόπνευστος or theópneustos), [theh-op'-nyoo-stos], literally means the breath or wind of God.

You and I may be inspired by a great photo, poem, or scenic view, but that's not what we're talking about here. When we say the Bible is inspired, we're saying it is God who breathed the writings into the author's heart and soul. The original words, phrases, and clauses join together to give us His message, and each portion of Scripture is there on purpose.

This is an important distinction from those who claim the Bible is a set of enriching stories like folklore, or a set of cultural values handed down through traditions. It is one of the ways you can tell if a person is a true follower of Christ or not. Do they believe in the inspiration of Scripture? But don't take my word for it, what does the Bible say about itself?

- *"For no prophecy was ever produced by the will of man, but men spoke from God as they were carried along by the Holy Spirit."* (2 Peter 1:21)
- *"The Spirit of the LORD spoke through me; His word was on my tongue."* (2 Samuel 23:2 NIV)
- *"The word of the LORD came directly to Ezekiel...the LORD's hand was upon him."* (Ezekiel 1:3 BSB)
- *"This is the word of the LORD that came to Micah."* (Micah 1:1 BSB)
- *"The Scripture had to be fulfilled which the Holy Spirit foretold through the mouth of David concerning Judas."* (Acts 1:16 BSB)
- *"God has fulfilled what He foretold through all the prophets, saying that His Christ would suffer."* (Acts 3:18 BSB)
- *"For whatever was written in former days was written for our instruction, that through endurance and through the encouragement of the Scriptures we might have hope."* (Romans 15:4)

The Bible is clear in its declaration of being a special text that was driven by God's inspiration through human authors. To say or believe otherwise is to be in direct contradiction to what the

Bible has to say about itself. That means to you and me that we can look to the Bible as the authority for daily living. As followers of Jesus, it's our map. It's our source of information on what to do and how to live.

Many people today are looking for how to live in a way that works. That's why God gave us the Bible. When you put its principles into practice, you'll discover your life finds true meaning, true significance, and true value. The reason you're experiencing emptiness, confusion, loneliness, fear, apathy, or any of these types of emotions is that you're trying to live your life off a map that doesn't provide you with the right direction. You end up lost when you look at the wrong map!

There are two more questions that I'd like to ask:

1. What does it mean to say the Bible is Infallible? (accurate and true)

2. What's the best way to Interpret the Bible? Interpretation (Exegesis vs Eisegesis), (Literal vs Allegorical). Author intent is better than reader response.

Next, let's move to the second part of this fantastic verse and discover the...

THE DESIGN OF GOD'S WORD
(HOW SHOULD I LIVE?)

"All Scripture is inspired by God and is useful for teaching the truth, rebuking error, correcting faults, and giving instruction for

right living, so that the person who serves God may be fully qualified and equipped to do every kind of good deed." (2 Timothy 3:16,17 GNT)

Almost everything in life has a design to it. Your house, car, clothes or jewelry were all designed by someone. There's a function or fashion to what's been designed. It serves a purpose. There's a reason for its existence. A wise person seeks to understand the design of a thing and then utilizes that design to his or her advantage.

It's the same thing with the Bible. In this "3:16 Passage" we discover four ways in which the Bible is designed to help us in our walk with Jesus. These are like the four directions on a map (North, South, East, and West). Just as you use four directions on a map to get where you want to go, you can use these four teaching points to direct you in the right course in your walk with Jesus.

How can we best use the Design of God's Word to help us in life?

"Teaching the truth"

The first way the Bible helps us is it teaches us the truth. Something interesting is going on here with this phrase. The emphasis here isn't in relation to mathematics, biology, or truth in general. The phrase is in connection to biblical truth which is called doctrine. Doctrine means "instruction, especially as it applies to lifestyle application." Everybody has a doctrine, everybody lives out their doctrine, the question is, is your doctrine truthful to the Bible?

This is significant as you build out the way you understand

God. How He communicates to you, and how you should best live the way He wants you to. When confronted with an unusual biblical interpretation or contradictions to a biblical worldview, having a strong and solid biblical doctrine helps you see through the smoke. You then develop a proper understanding of a particular issue or choice of lifestyle. You can then stand on that because it matches God's point of view on the subject. It helps you to spot false teachers and those attempting to take you down a road that's not on God's map for your life.

The Bible tells us, "Keep a close watch on how you live and on your teaching. Stay true to what is right for the sake of your own salvation and the salvation of those who hear you." (1 Timothy 4:16)

"Rebuking error"

A second way the Bible helps you is by rebuking errors in your life. That simply means to bring something to your attention so that it convicts you. It causes you to change paths. Head down a new road. Turn around. The Bible doesn't sugarcoat who we are. It calls us out on behavior that is not godly. These are the things that pull us away from God and what He wants for our life. When we are faced with that information, we have a choice. We can take the information and use it to make a change, or we can ignore it at our own expense.

As a pastor it's part of my job to teach the whole counsel of God and to, *"Teach what is appropriate to sound doctrine."* (Titus 2:1 NIV) It's the responsibility of Christian leaders to teach as Paul taught the leaders in Ephesus, *"For I did not shrink from declaring to you the whole counsel of God."* (Acts 20:27)

But don't miss this part. Another point of application is to learn how to build a solid wall, a fortress of protection from yourself. The Bible gets real with us. *"No prophecy of Scripture comes from someone's own interpretation."* (2 Peter 1:20) In other words, don't twist the Bible to make it fit what you want it to say. Let the Bible stand for itself. Let it change you.

"Correcting faults"

A third way the Bible helps you is by restoring your life. The original language for this phrase, "correcting faults," means "to straighten up, lift (set) up, make straight."[51]

One time Jesus was teaching and a disabled person was nearby. The Bible says He called her over and then *"He placed His hands on her, and at once she stood up straight and praised God."* (Luke 13:13 CEV) The idea of standing up straight in this story is the same idea being expressed in this "3:16 Passage." But instead of standing up straight physically, the Bible is talking about restoring us and causing us to stand up straight spiritually. In our ethics, in our character, in the way we handle our business. In the way, we treat our family and neighbors. He wants to heal your spiritual disability so you can live for Him.

Jesus said it this way, in referring to the religious experts of His day, *"Their worship is a farce, for they teach man-made ideas as commands from God."* (Mark 7:7) I don't know anyone who wants to be known as a farce to Jesus. That's pretty serious.

God provides you with a tool that helps you not become a bogus person or a person who becomes a spiritual fake. The Bible is a tool that provides a way to help you correct your faults so you can stand straight for God's kingdom. He uses the Bible to restore you and turn you into the person He has created you to be.

"Giving instruction for right living"

A fourth way the Bible helps you is by giving instruction for right living. We're tempted to make the Bible fit what we want. We want the Bible to fit nicely into our cultural norms. We don't want to offend people. If the Bible offends them, we try to bend over backward to interpret the biblical text in a way that is comforting for the issue.

The problem with this idea is when a culture changes so does the meaning of Scripture. If we do that, then our view of God becomes whatever we want Him to be. Instead of us being created in the image of God, we end up creating God in our own image. And that, my friend, is a whole 'nother level of crazy.

There's a powerful passage that tells us, *"If anyone teaches a different doctrine and does not agree with the sound words of our Lord Jesus Christ and the teaching that accords with godliness, 4he is puffed up with conceit and understands nothing."* (1 Timothy 6:3-4)

I'm thankful God doesn't leave us to ourselves. He intervenes so you can be transformed. Sometimes that transformation is fast and sometimes it takes time, but the question is are you putting yourself in a place that allows the Bible to instruct you in the way you should live?

Three ways you can do that is by coming to church regularly to hear and interact with God's Word. Get into a Life Group so you can talk with others about your journey. And begin some type of daily quiet time with God. If you do those three simple things, you'll see your spiritual life flourish.

Finally, let's look at...

THE DIRECTIVE OF GOD'S WORD
(WHERE AM I GOING?)

"All Scripture is inspired by God and is useful for teaching the truth, rebuking error, correcting faults, and giving instruction for right living, so that the person who serves God may be fully qualified and equipped to do every kind of good deed." (2 Timothy 3:16,17 GNT)

Have you ever seen something new and didn't know what it was for? You may remember when cars made a change from putting a key into the ignition to just pushing a button to start it. One time I borrowed a car from a family member and I remember the first time I experienced that. I kept pushing the button and pushing the button until it registered that I also had to push on the brake pedal at the same time. The designers of the car knew exactly what they were doing and the reason behind this new design. I just needed to catch up with the designers.

This idea of design is obviously seen in various forms of art as well, especially statues and stonework. Mount Rushmore began construction in 1927 and ended in 1941 with a total cost of one million dollars for the project. Most people are familiar with the half-completed image carved into the South Dakota granite. But many have never seen the model of what the complete product is supposed to look like. The halfway completed structure is based on a fully completed model.

The Bible describes our life as being in constant growth and transformation. Sometimes we feel like we're only half-completed.

We learn from this "3:16 Passage" that God provides His Word so we can grow into the person He wants us to be. He has a completed version of who He wants us to be. It's as if God has a sculpture in Heaven and this model is the fullness of the directive. *"For God knew His people in advance, and He chose them to become like His Son."* (Romans 8:29)

What is the Bible's directive as it relates to your life?

"Fully Qualified"

When you apply God's Word to your life you end up being fully qualified. The idea of being fully qualified means to be fitted for duty. It means you have the character, quality, temperament, and experience to do the tasks God has for your life. God is working on you every day. He has a complete picture of you and how He wants to best utilize your life for His kingdom. In this overarching plan, as you continue to apply God's Word to your life and allow it to mold and shape you and your decisions, you will slowly but surely be transformed into the image of Jesus. So many people are scared that God is going to put them in a situation that is overwhelming. Fear seizes their heart, and they don't take that next step of faith. Don't do that. As you pour into the Word of God, He will make sure you're fully qualified to handle life.

"Equipped"

Additionally, when you apply God's Word to your life you end up being equipped. This sounds like the last idea. But in the original language, this means to furnish perfectly. When you buy a new house, you have to furnish it. When you have a new baby, you have to furnish the house with all sorts of new items. According to parents.com there are 6 steps to babyproofing your house. We're the same way. When you come to Christ, you're like a baby spiritually and God begins the process of perfectly furnishing your life. In the initial stages of your growth God puts up barriers and guard rails, but as you get older and further along God provides the continuing things necessary to grow. The Bible is saying that when you use the application of Scripture to your life, you're perfectly furnishing your life with what you need.

Think of it this way, just because an NCAA college basketball team is fully qualified to be in this year's March Madness tournament, it doesn't mean that team is fully equipped to win it all. The Bible is teaching us here that not only will you be fully qualified, you will also be furnished perfectly to be a winner on God's team.

As God chisels away the rough edges of your life know He is molding and shaping you into the person He's designed you to be and become. He's never done with you. There's always work to do. The question always is, are you up for the confrontation from the chisel? When God's chisel shows up, something's getting chipped away. But the good news is whatever is being chipped away is simply making room for whatever is underneath and that's the part God is wanting to display.

It brings us to ask, do you trust the work of your Creator?

We have looked at the Description, Design, and Directive of God's Word. He is All-Knowing.

CONCLUSION

This chapter's attribute: God is All-Knowing.

The theological term for this is omniscience. Omni means all and science means knowledge. When someone says, "I believe in science" you can say, I do too. In fact, I believe in the God of science. He's the God of all knowledge.

Because God is all-knowing, this can help you when you're looking for answers to life's questions. We tend to base our solutions and answers on feelings, but God's knowledge is greater than what something feels like. *"God is greater than our feelings, and He knows everything."* (1 John 3:20)

He knows about the smallest details, *"Not a single sparrow can fall to the ground without your Father knowing it. And the very hairs on your head are all numbered."* (Matthew 10:29-30)

He knows everything from the beginning to the end of history. *"I am God, and there is none like Me, declaring the end from the beginning and from ancient times things not yet done, saying, 'My counsel shall stand, and I will accomplish all My purpose.'"* (Isaiah 46:9-10)

Yet in all this, He knows every thought of the human heart, *"You know what I am going to say even before I say it, LORD."* (Psalm 139:4)

Knowing God is All-Knowing brings the follower of Jesus incredible confidence and peace. You can be secure in the knowledge that He will never abandon you as you remain steadfast in Him. An all-knowing God possesses limitless power,

He has been aware of you since the beginning of time, even before the universe was created. God knew every detail about you, including where you would exist and with whom you would interact.

He even anticipated your mistakes, with all the consequences and selfishness, yet He still embraced you with love, placing His mark upon you and leading you toward His love through Jesus Christ. *"Even before He made the world, God loved us and chose us in Christ to be holy and without fault in His eyes. ⁵God decided in advance to adopt us into His own family by bringing us to Himself through Jesus Christ. This is what He wanted to do, and it gave Him great pleasure."* (Ephesians 1:4-5)

You may know Kelsey Grammer as Dr. Frasier Crane on the popular sitcoms Cheers and Frasier. The Juilliard-trained actor has a background in theater, film, and television. His latest project, "Jesus Revolution," has become Lionsgate studio's highest-grossing film since 2019. Expected to earn around $6 or $7 million in ticket sales, it has already surpassed $40 million at the box office.

What you may not know is that behind Grammer's success, lies a history of loss, addiction and broken relationships. When he was 13, his father was shot and killed. Seven years later, his younger sister was kidnapped and murdered. Five years later, his half-brothers died in a suspected shark attack. He struggled with alcohol and drug addictions for years.

Grammer's faith was also tested as he grappled with anger and guilt over his sister's death, but even though he admitted 'losing his faith' he eventually came back around to Jesus and realized

God had been guiding Him all along.

According to Grammer, his life experiences prepared him for his role in the film. Grammer said, "It strikes me, you know, I probably have been preparing for this all my life, honestly."

God guided the Israelites by a cloud during the day and fire by night. He guided the early church by sending the right people at the right time. Through it all, God was present.

Kelsey's story, though unique, is like each of our stories. God has been walking alongside us through the good times and the bad, times of great faith and great failures. And as we acknowledge that, God will use our stories to draw others to Himself.

God is guiding each of us into a new life in Him where our story and His faithfulness come together in the love that we share with others.

Chapter 10

The God Who Challenges You

Revelation 3:16

Attribute: God is Holy

Craig Groeschel, a friend I met at a pastor's retreat, shares a story about an interaction he had with the inventor of the Koosh ball, a man named Mark. They were both at the same family camp and were enjoying time in the swimming pool with their families. Mark dared Craig to hold his breath underwater for one minute. Craig is a competitive guy, so he took a deep breath and at 40 seconds Craig his lungs were burning so much he was rededicating his life to Jesus. At 60 seconds he exploded up out of the water as if he were a synchronized swimmer at the Olympics.

Mark challenged Groeschel again, "I bet you could do it twice as long if you do what I tell you. Before you go under, breathe in and out deeply four times. Then when your lungs start to burn, let a little air out and it will trick your brain into thinking you are about to give it more oxygen. Your brain does not understand what your body is capable of."

This time when Craig went underwater, he listened to the coaching and encouragement Mark was shouting out to him every 15 seconds or so. Craig held his breath for two minutes and 45 seconds. He decided, "there was way more inside of me than I ever understood."

I want to help you understand that God has put way more inside of you than you realize. And because you serve a God who loves you, He's not afraid to challenge you into spiritual greatness.

It's easy to forget about the things that matter most. We tend to get caught up in the everyday problems and challenges of life. We tend to get disconnected from our faith as we focus on things that don't really matter. Maybe you're feeling lost or disconnected from your faith. I have good news for you. God wants to provide a wake-up call that can help you reconnect with your spiritual life.

Revelation 3:16 says, *"But since you are like lukewarm water, neither hot nor cold, I will spit you out of my mouth!"* This verse reminds us that it's not enough to go through the motions of faith - we need to be fully committed and passionate about our beliefs. If we are lukewarm or indifferent, we risk losing touch with the very things that give our lives meaning and eternal purpose.

Whether you are struggling to find your spiritual path, or simply feeling disconnected from your faith, Revelation 3:16 can be a powerful call to action. With courage and conviction you can find the strength and guidance you need to live a life full of faith and with divine purpose.

I want to show you the five ways God challenges you in our final "3:16 Passage."

First, let's take a look at…

GOD'S CHALLENGE TO BE RELEVANT

"But since you are like lukewarm water, neither hot nor cold, I will spit you out of my mouth!" (Revelation 3:16)

Businesses throughout the world strive to maintain relevance. Sales and marketing teams hold meetings and strategy sessions. Research teams search through data, surveys, and consumer responses. All in the hope that their product or service can maintain significance and connection with consumers. Actors, singers, and entertainers continually reinvent themselves to stay relevant. If a business or media personality falls behind, they lose their influence and eventually run the risk of disappearing back into society or losing their needed revenue to maintain profitability.

Can that happen to you spiritually? Can you be in a place where your spiritual life is running on all cylinders and God is using your life to impact your world in a powerful way and then something happens, and you fall off? Can a Christian simply fail to launch any sort of spiritual relevance or impact at all?

Let's provide some background. The "3:16 passage" we're looking at is part of a letter that was written by a man name John. He was one of the original 12 disciples and is also the same person who wrote the gospel of John and 1, 2, and 3 John as well. He was an Apostle and one of Jesus' inner circle. He referred to himself as "the disciple whom Jesus loved" in John 13:23.

The letter we're exploring today was written to a group of Christians in the city of Laodicea. This letter is one of seven letters that John wrote to an entire group of churches in Asia Minor or modern-day Turkey. The book of Revelation (chapters 1 thru 3) opens with seven letters to seven churches. Each of the seven letters is a prophetic word from Jesus through the Holy Spirit who inspired John to write to these churches. N.T. scholar, Craig Keener explains,

Laodicea is close to ten miles west of Colossae and six miles south of Hierapolis. Laodicea boasted great resources but had a poor water supply. Ancient sources state that it was full of sediment, and excavation of the city's terra cotta pipes reveal thick lime deposits, which suggest heavy contamination. Because Laodicea had to pipe in its water, it grew lukewarm by the time of its arrival. The point of lukewarm water is simply that it is disgusting, in contrast to the more directly useful "hot" and "cold" water. Jesus finds the church in Laodicea to be other than what He desires. In today's English, He is telling the self-satisfied church in Laodicea: "I want water that will refresh me, but you remind me instead of the water you always complain about.[52]

The challenge from God to the Laodiceans is straightforward. Be useful for God's kingdom. When the Bible says Jesus would rather you be hot or cold, it's not referring to your spiritual temperature but rather your usefulness. The hot water piped in from the city of Hierapolis was useful for healing and restoration. The cold water piped in from Colossae was useful for refreshment and quenching people's thirst. Lukewarm water was useless.

The iPhone is a beautiful product, but it's little more than a paperweight if it's not connected to a network. That's your story too. You're a beautiful part of God's creation, but if you're not connected to God's network, you're not achieving the best God has for you.

It's easy for us to lose connection with God if we are not careful. Problems, issues, or disappointments can all fight against us and cause us to pull back or disconnect from the Body of Christ. I want to encourage you to not allow the negative things in life to pull you away or turn you away from God.

Stay faithful, engaged, involved, connected, and useful to God. When you do that, it's the first step to pulling out of you more than you ever thought possible.

Next, let's take a look at...

GOD'S CHALLENGE TO BE REAL

"You say, 'I am rich. I have everything I want. I don't need a thing!' And you don't realize that you are wretched and miserable and poor and blind and naked." (Revelation 3:17)

The US Census Bureau's new data shows the average household income in America is just over $100,000 per year.[53] Historically speaking, there's never been a greater amount of sheer dollars moving through the homes of individuals of a nation since the dawn of humanity. Additionally, American households collectively held well over $98 trillion of wealth in 2018.[54]

These enormous resources should lead us to a very happy and

satisfied culture, wouldn't you agree? But we're not happy. And we are not satisfied. Consider this, according to recent annual statistics from the American Society of Plastic Surgeons, nearly $16.7 billion was spent on cosmetic procedures in the U.S. in 2020.[55] What are we trying to hide?

As a culture, we're spending billions of dollars on procedures to modify our image. Don't get me wrong, in many cases, these procedures are completely necessary like in the case of a burn victim or similar situations. However, we all know that for the most part, the majority of these procedures are for "cosmetic" purposes only.

We have vanity plates for our vehicles. We have software designed to alter our pictures so we look better. We hire coaches and consultants for eating, working out, building wealth, career advancement, or any other topic you can think of.

We've become masters at covering up or attempting to fix our flaws. We bury or ignore tough conversations needed to help our relationships flourish and grow. We push off our responsibilities to a professional therapy class thereby excusing the ramifications of our actions. We pontificate about our expertise in an area of study and exclaim there's no need for God. We treat others as less than ourselves through pride, ego, and sarcasm.

Yet as a nation of people with resources and education far greater than any society in history, we are more miserable than ever before.

Political anger, cultural divisiveness, depression, anxiety, substance abuse, divorce, broken homes, family relationships on edge, increasing single-parent homes, and record homelessness, are all on the rise and none of it shows any sign of slowing down. What's the answer to our misery?

According to this "3:16 passage," with apathy comes spiritual blindness. When we become indifferent to God, we are unable to see our true condition. That's what happened to the Christians and people of Laodicea and that's what's happening in our nation today.

This isn't a new thing. One time in the Old Testament a similar thing happened. The prophet Ezekiel shared a message to the king of Tyre, a very wealthy city during his day. *"Yes, your wisdom has made you very rich, and your riches have made you very proud."* (Ezekiel 28:5) All the wealth and knowledge made the king proud, and God eventually removed him from his man-made throne. He let all the success go to his head and forgot how He got there in the first place.

But this doesn't have to happen to you. You can't change the entire culture, but you can be responsible for your individual relationship with God and how you interact with the people He connects you with.

Verse 17 teaches that God loves you enough to challenge you to get real with yourself and your situation. The situation is that you and I desperately need God. We need Jesus to forgive us, redeem us, and restore us. No matter my earthly wealth, spiritually I'm a mess without Christ and so are you. We need Him.

During one of Jesus' most famous sermons, the Sermon on the Mount, He told us, *"Blessed are the poor in spirit, for theirs is the kingdom of heaven."* (Matthew 5:3) To be "poor in spirit" does not refer to being materially poor, but rather it is a spiritual attitude. It means to recognize and acknowledge one's own spiritual poverty, to be humble before God, and have a deep sense of dependence on Him for all things.

In other words, Jesus is saying that those who get real with their need for God, who acknowledge their own spiritual poverty, and turn to Him with a humble and contrite heart, will be blessed and receive the kingdom of heaven. This attitude of humility and dependence on God is essential for true spiritual growth and transformation. It's the second way you pull way more out of yourself than you ever thought possible.

Next, let's take a look at....

GOD'S CHALLENGE TO BE RELIANT

"So I advise you to buy gold from me—gold that has been purified by fire. Then you will be rich. Also buy white garments from me so you will not be shamed by your nakedness, and ointment for your eyes so you will be able to see." (Rev. 3:18)

This third challenge is counterintuitive because we live in a self-reliant culture. Pull yourself up by your bootstraps. Trust your instincts. Trust no one. Take care of yourself first. These and similar ideologies are deeply embedded in our culture.

Thirty-nine year-old actress Felicity Jones sums up the view of many when she says, "I think that my parent's divorce gave me a very strong sense of self-reliance and independence. I realized that I needed to make sure I could support myself because you don't know what's going to happen in the future."[56]

While there's nothing wrong with taking personal responsibility for your future, if you apply this same standard to your spiritual life, it can wreak havoc upon your relationship with God.

In the letter to the church in Laodicea, Jesus advises them to "buy" three things: gold, white garments, and ointment. To "buy" is a reference to reliance. For example, as a baby you relied upon your parents for all your needs. As an adult, you rely upon the military to safeguard peace within our borders.

Gold is a reference to that which lasts. At the judgment seat of Christ, all our deeds will be put to the test. They will be refined by the fire of God's judgment. *"On the judgment day, fire will reveal what kind of work each builder has done. The fire will show if a person's work has any value. [14]If the work survives, that builder will receive a reward. [15]But if the work is burned up, the builder will suffer great loss."* (1 Corinthians 3:13-15)

The judgment seat of Christ, also known as the Bema Seat judgment, is a term used to describe the judgment Christians will face after we die. We will stand before Jesus and give an account of our lives as believers. This judgment is not a judgment of condemnation, but a judgment of rewards and accountability for believers.

The Bible teaches that judgment for a Christian happens at what is called the Judgment Seat of Christ. At that event, we will give an account of how we have conducted our lives and used the resources and opportunities God has given us. This includes thoughts, words, and actions, as well as the stewardship of our time, talents, and resources.

The Bible teaches we will be rewarded based on our faithfulness to Christ and our obedience to His will. These rewards may include crowns, positions of authority, and other privileges in the eternal kingdom of God.

It is important to note that the judgment seat of Christ is separate from what the Bible describes as the Great White Throne judgment, which is a judgment of condemnation for those who have rejected Christ as Savior. For believers, the judgment seat of Christ is a time of accountability and reward, where we will receive the fullness of God's grace and mercy.

White garments are a reference to righteousness. The Bible teaches that if you are in Christ you are clothed in His righteousness, *"I will greatly rejoice in the LORD; my soul shall exult in my God, for He has clothed me with the garments of salvation; He has covered me with the robe of righteousness."* (Isaiah 61:10) In contrast to the righteousness of Christ, our righteous actions amount to nothing.

A few chapters later the prophet Isaiah reminds us, *"We are all infected and impure with sin. When we display our righteous deeds, they are nothing but filthy rags. Like autumn leaves, we wither and fall, and our sins sweep us away like the wind."* (Isaiah 64:6)

The ointment is a reference to seeing life through God's wisdom. Because of our limited capacity, we simply cannot gain the fullness of insight regarding the things right in front of us. We need God's help to provide insight and wisdom. The Bible encourages us, *"For a man's ways are before the eyes of the LORD, and He ponders all his paths."* (Proverbs 5:21)

How do you rely upon God in a self-reliant world? You start by reassessing what you value. And then You trust Him for your salvation as you seek Him for guidance. It's the third way you pull way more out of yourself than you ever thought possible.

Next, let's take a look at....

GOD'S CHALLENGE TO REPENT

"I correct and discipline everyone I love. So be diligent and turn from your indifference." (Revelation 3:19)

In this context, the challenge to the Laodiceans was to repent (or turn away) from their lukewarm attitude toward God. They were ineffective in their community. They were self-centered in their outlook. They were indifferent in their walk with Jesus. They were weak in their spiritual life. Jesus clearly tells them, because of His great love for them, He is challenging them to turn around and get back on the right path. Stop being lethargic in your faith. Get back into the gym and start flexing and working out those spiritual muscles again.

Repentance is an interesting word in our day. If you want to get someone fired up, just tell them they need to repent. You'll get all kinds of interesting responses. What causes that kind of reaction?

I think it's because nobody likes to be told what to do. Have you ever seen two people in an argument in public? Clearly, someone's wrong yet they'll stand there for minutes just arguing about some silly point nobody cares about. Does anyone really care if the grocery cart was returned to the cart caddy? But because neither person wants to be seen as being wrong, they just stand there and continue to yell. It's rather fascinating to tell you the truth. Finally, the police arrive to break it up.

We're seeing this more and more in our society, from courtrooms to classrooms people are digging in. Nobody wants to admit they're wrong. When you adopt this type of viewpoint, it creates a stalemate between you and the person you're speaking with. That's why letting go of your pride and taking up the challenge to repent is so valuable. Especially as it relates to your relationship with God.

God doesn't want you to turn away from your sinful actions and attitudes because He wants to be right and you to be wrong. Let's give God a bit more credit than that. He's way more mature than we are. This whole invitation to turn away from your indifference or ungodly actions is not for Him to be right it's for you to be made right!

As you engage in actions and activities that are ungodly, you're only damaging yourself. God is inviting you to wake up and start walking in the newness of life. A life He has planned out for you. But you can't begin that new life if you're stuck in behaviors and attitudes that are contrary to the love of Jesus. So He invites you to turn away from the old ways and walk forward in a new way… a better way.

In the book of Acts, chapter 11, Peter returns to Jerusalem from a recent trip to Joppa and Caesarea. He had to give a report to the church leaders about what God was doing in other parts of their region. The good news of Jesus was spreading fast, and many people were receiving Jesus and repenting. While in Caesarea, there was a group of Gentiles who received the message of salvation and became followers of Jesus.

When Peter returned to share the news, here's what the leaders in Jerusalem said, *"We can see that God has also given the Gentiles the privilege of repenting of their sins and receiving eternal life."* (Acts 11:18) Did you catch that? Here's a group of people that understood this divine challenge to repent. They understood it correctly. It's a privilege to repent because it allows you to receive eternal life!

Do you need to turn away from something in your life? If so, go ahead and make the decision right now. Purpose in your heart to turn away from that action or attitude and turn to back to Christ. As you accept this challenge to repent, it's the fourth way you pull way more out of yourself than you ever thought possible.

Finally, let's look at.....

GOD'S CHALLENGE TO BE IN RELATIONSHIP

"Look! I stand at the door and knock. If you hear my voice and open the door, I will come in, and we will share a meal together as friends." (Revelation 3:20)

Imagine for a moment the opportunity to sit down with a few of the wealthiest people in the world. Topping the list this year are Elon Musk, Jeff Bezos, Bill Gates, and Warren Buffet. They have a combined net worth of $600 billion.[57] During your brief conversation, all four decide they really like you. They think you were pretty cool. At the end of the conversation, they invite you over to their home for dinner anytime you like, and they want you to consider them your friend. You even exchange personal cell phone numbers.

I bet you'd think that was amazing and that your life might be a bit different from here on out because you now have four friends in very high places. You have access to something you didn't have before. In fact, go ahead and pick your favorite athlete, singer, leader, actor or actress and run the same thought experiment and I bet you'd come to the same conclusion, your life would be better if you were friends with people of influence.

Here's what's interesting, no matter how many famous or influential people you have a connection with, they all pale in comparison to having a personal relationship with God. You and I have the opportunity to have a personal and individual connection with the Creator of everything. His net worth cannot be calculated. $600 billion is like one small grain of sand in a galaxy full of sand. There's no way to compute His resources, power, influence, and authority. And yet, this Creator invites you, yes you, into a personal relationship with Him.

In our "3:16 Passage," the Christians in Laodicea were lukewarm, they were apathetic toward Jesus. Yet, because of His great love for them, He invites them to open the door and start again. It's the same for you. I don't know where you are in your spiritual life. Maybe you were once on fire for Jesus. Maybe you were connected in a stronger and more vibrant way. Maybe you've grown lukewarm and indifferent. If that's you, know this,

Jesus is standing at the door knocking. He's saying, *"Look! I stand at the door and knock. If you hear my voice and open the door, I will come in, and we will share a meal together as friends."* (Revelation 3:20)

This verse is often used as an evangelistic appeal, yet what's going on here is Jesus going after believers who have turned their back on Him. Rather than Jesus turning His back on them, He goes after them. If they take God up on His four previous challenges, He will share a meal with them, which is a Middle Eastern word picture speaking of a closeness of relationship. Have you been indifferent in your relationship with God? Can you hear Jesus knocking today? Can you sense His presence? Can you hear His voice? If so, why not simply open the door of your heart and begin again.

Peter encourages the listeners of his second sermon, *"Repent, then, and turn to God, so that your sins may be wiped out, that times of refreshing may come from the Lord."* (Acts 3:19 NIV) This word refreshing is ἀνάψυξις anápsyxis, [pron. an-aps'-ook-sis] and it means to experience a recovery of breath (figuratively), or to experience revival (to be revived). This is the only instance in the Bible that this word is used. In this case, it's the presence of God that revives or awakens the heart and soul by causing your spirit to breathe again.

That's what God wants to do in your life. He wants to awaken your soul with His presence as you open the door and invite Him into your life again. As you accept this challenge to receive Him, it's the fifth way you pull way more out of yourself than you ever thought possible.

This brings us to our final attribute...

CONCLUSION

This Chapter's Attribute: God is Holy

Some people wonder why God requires humanity to repent and turn away from sinful behavior. The reason is that He is holy. Holy means pure, sacred, and set apart. He is endlessly, always perfect. If God didn't require humanity to turn from their sin it would be a contradiction to His very nature. He couldn't share their company.

Revelation 4:8 tells us, *"Holy, holy, holy is the Lord God Almighty."* (NIV)

Jesus mentions the perfection of God, *"You therefore must be perfect, as your heavenly Father is perfect."* (Matthew 5:48)

Because God desires a personal relationship with us, His love wrapped inside of holiness brings us to a place of remorse for our actions. Oswald Chambers writes, "When we preach the love of God there is a danger of forgetting that the Bible reveals not first the love of God but the intense, blazing holiness of God, with His love at the center of that holiness." When you first become a Christian, you don't notice all the little things that are in contradiction with God's holiness. But as you grow closer to Him, and the light of God's presence shines brighter and brighter it's like drawing closer to an immense light and you notice the little things you want to remove from your life so you can better match the character and nature of your Savior and Lord.

The holiness of God is another way God draws more out of you than you thought possible.

In 2016, 14-year-old Ashley Jones' father died suddenly of a heart attack while he was at her soccer practice. "There was a lot of sadness, but we never felt anger. We knew my dad was whole again, that he wasn't hurting. I had the hope that I'd see him again, in Heaven."

That summer, friends invited her family to go hiking and off-roading. Tragedy struck again. As she was riding on an ATV, the driver took a corner too fast, tipped over crushing her right arm which had to be amputated.

Ashley asked God for a glimpse of His plan for her life: God, this happened for a reason, and I'm trusting you to show me what's next.

A week later, Bethany Hamilton, a Christian surfer who'd lost her arm to a shark attack at age 13, invited her to a camp she'd started for girls with amputations which teaches them to adapt to their new life after trauma.

That summer before she was meant to compete again for her high school team, she dislocated her left knee and tore her meniscus and her ACL.

Once again, she adapted. She rehabbed her knee and, in August 2018, found a camp focused on triathlon sports and began training. In the spring of 2019, she joined the Valor High track team as a junior and the cross-country team as a senior.

Today you will find Ashley running on High Point University's Track and Field Team.

How could Ashley push through and succeed after so many setbacks?

She says her faith is what gives her story its redemption. "I think the good that's come out of these events has shown me the good of God," she says. "I might have been the most underqualified person in track, cross-country, and triathlons, but my experiences have shown me that you're a lot stronger than you think you are. When God says He will bring you into a new time of joy, it's true." For Ashley, good is behind, and greatness is ahead.

Friend, how about you? Are you ready to embrace the greatness ahead of you by putting your whole trust in Jesus Christ? This is your 3:16 moment.

Conclusion

We have completed our grand tour of the Bible's 3:16 verses. But any foray into the Bible, the Word of God, always feels like scratching the surface of timeless stories of men and women just like us who were surprised by grace and transformed by the truths they were living out.

Exploring the nature of God is like wandering through a national forest. The beauty is overwhelming, but we need signposts to make our way through the immensity of it. The tendency is to think of God as an impersonal force behind the world we see, something too big or mysterious to be known or, at worst, a giant to be feared. But God is a Someone, not a something.

The 3:16 verses have shown us God is personal and knowable. Most importantly, God is characterized not only by high minded virtues, but because of Jesus, He is down to earth. The Bible calls that being incarnate. He is knowable. Like the old story about the little boy who was being tucked into bed during a storm. He was reluctant to let his mother leave and she assured him that Jesus loved him and would look after him. The little boy said, "I want somebody with skin on!"

Jesus is God with skin on, and each of us is Jesus with skin on to those around us. The 3:16 verses tell us a lot about God. Now it is up to each of us to be mirrors of Jesus to our families, friends, workplace associates and a watching world.

Conclusion

Carl Gregg tells the story of being in seminary and learning about the most well-known of the 3:16 verses, John 3:16. The one we covered in an earlier chapter where God SO loved the world...that He gave. He describes his discovery about the importance of a word:

"Toward the middle of my first semester of Greek, our professor asked us to make an original translation of John 3:16 as if we were unfamiliar with the famous verse. We quickly saw the point of the assignment. The very first word of John 3:16 in Greek is *outos*. In the vast majority of English Bibles, this word is translated as "so," as in "God so loved the world." The problem is that many of us hear that "so" in the wrong way. We hear it in terms of degree: "God didn't just love the world; God loved the world a LOT." But that's not the way John meant it. Another meaning of the English word "so" is the sense of "in this way" or "in this manner." Try to hear the "so" in that sense: "God so loved the world. God loved the world in this way. God so loved the world. God loved the world in this manner."[58]

In learning about—making mental assent to the goodness of God—His trustworthiness, His wisdom, the fact that He has our back in life, we now get to work that down into our lives. Deep into our spirit where anxiety and bitterness and cynicism live. That is the challenge. To allow that truth to transform us all the way. Then to go out into a dangerous and unpredictable world and love others THAT WAY. The way Jesus loved.

You see, Jesus is described as the way, the truth and the life. When we read the New Testament, we see the way He interacted with others. He knew when someone needed "tough love," even a kick in the pants, and He knew when they were broken and needed a non-judgmental embrace.

That is what this trip through the 3:16 verses has been about. Knowing God, knowing ourselves, and being honest with Him to help us become the person we know we already are and yet are becoming. In taking this journey together we have explored the qualities of God and encountered someone whose actual nature is in contrast to our mental image. Someone who is infinitely wise, loving, and just. We have witnessed His unwavering presence, His boundless mercy, and His unshakeable faithfulness. In contemplating these qualities, we find an invitation to trust God – really trust Him – and model ourselves after Him.

Trust in God is not blind faith but an acknowledgment of His character. We can trust Him because His wisdom surpasses our limited understanding. When we face challenges and uncertainties, we can rely on His guidance, knowing He sees the bigger picture and works all things together for our ultimate good.

God's love is a constant source of reassurance. It is a love that knows no boundaries, embracing us in our brokenness and lifting us up in times of despair. We can trust Him to be there in our moments of joy and sorrow, offering solace, comfort, and unwavering support. His love compels us to extend kindness and compassion to others, modeling ourselves after His example. Is there someone in your life who is hurting who requires a 3:16 response? If you're like me, I'm sure many people come to mind. Perhaps you need to take an honest look at your relationships one by one and see how implementing the 3:16 verses can heal them.

Charles Spurgeon, a famous preacher from the nineteenth

century said, "God is too good to be unkind and He is too wise to be mistaken. And when we cannot trace His hand, we must trust His heart."

God's justice provides us with the assurance that the evil we witness, the cruelty and unfairness of it all, will be addressed. In a world often marred by injustice and inequality, we can find solace in knowing that God is the ultimate judge. We can trust Him to bring justice to every situation, even when it seems elusive in the present moment. But His justice is tempered with the mercy of a parent.

As we strive to model ourselves after God, we are called to live out those qualities in our own lives. But how do we do that? By getting up each day and praying, reflecting, studying the Bible and being 3:16 people every single day.

Timothy Keller, pastor, theologian, and Christian apologist, recently died. In an interview with Outreach Magazine in 2021, he shares this beautiful story:

There is a famous short story by J.R.R. Tolkien called *Leaf by Niggle*. Niggle is a painter who spends his entire life trying to paint a mural of a tree. By the end of his life, he has only gotten one leaf completed. Then he dies. But when he gets to heaven, he sees the tree that was always there in his mind. That is the way of the Christian. My son Jonathan is an urban planner. In his mind, he has all these exciting ideas about what a great city would look like. Well, as a Christian, he realizes that in his entire life he may only get one "leaf" done of his beautiful vision. We all face that reality. Nevertheless, we live with the hope that there will be a tree. There will be a city. There is going to be a just society.

Beauty will be here. Poverty and war will be gone. We are not the saviors. Instead, hope can set us free from both the despair of nihilism and the naivety of utopianism.[59]

My prayer for you is that the words you have read will provide another stepping stone in your life. Or perhaps something you read, a word, a thought, will be a catalyst for change. More than anything, I pray you will know God and believe what the apostle Paul wrote when he said…that He who began a good work in you will bring it to completion at the day of Jesus Christ. (Philippians 1:6) That He will make sense of your life, show you that the puzzle pieces like 3:16 verses, fit together. That He will make your existence meaningful as you live out your 3:16 life every single day. Are you ready to embody that redemptive challenge? We can do it together.

About the Author

T.K. Anderson has served in pastoral ministry for over two decades. He is passionate about teaching the Word of God, using apologetics to answer the questions that often go unasked. He is the author of *Pocket Theology, Faith Jump, and Freedom: Living Above Your Circumstances.*. He holds a bachelor's degree in Theological Studies from North Central University, a master's degree in Christian Apologetics from Biola University and is completing his D.Min. at Southern California Seminary. Mr. Anderson holds dual memberships with the Evangelical Theological and Philosophical Societies. He currently serves as the Lead Pastor of **Compass Church** in Salinas, CA.

Notes

[1] Adapted from Robert Morgan, *The Red Sea Rules* (Nashville, TN: Thomas Nelson, 2001), 7.

[2] https://stephenmillerbooks.com/more-evidence-for-the-miracle-jordan-river-stops/

[3] https://science.howstuffworks.com/rain-other-planets.htm

[4] Adapted from Max Lucado, *Facing Your Giants* (Nashville, TN: Thomas Nelson, 2006), 165.

[5] Max Lucado, *Facing Your Giants* (Nashville, TN: Thomas Nelson, 2006), 166.

[6] Mark Batterson, Wild Goose Chase (Colorado Springs, CO: Multnomah Books, 2008), 29.

[7] Adapted from Mark Batterson's *Wild Goose Chase*, 27.

[8] https://www.upi.com/Archives/1984/11/06/A-man-who-confessed-to-a-15-year-old-murder-last/7113468565200/

[9] Adapted from David Jeremiah's *Slaying the Giants in Your Life* (Nashville, TN: Thomas Nelson, 2001), 86.

[10] Kyle Idleman, *not a fan. daily devotional* (Grand Rapids, MI: Zondervan, 2016), 17.

[11] Terry Crist, *Learning The Language of Babylon* (Grand Rapids, MI: Chosen Books, 2001), 41.

[12] Charles Swindoll, *The Tale of the Tardy Oxcart* (Nashville, TN: Word Publishing, 1998), 631.

[13] https://www.turnbacktogod.com/story-in-the-court-with-jesus-as-my-lawyer/, accessed Jan 26, 2023.

[14] https://guideposts.org/inspiring-stories/stories-of-faith-and-hope/meeting-mother-teresa-led-him-to-a-life-of-service/

[15] https://convoyofhope.org/in-the-news/forbes-top-100-charities/

[16] https://money.usnews.com/investing/news/articles/2023-01-26/wells-fargo-ceo-scharfs-2022-pay-unchanged-at-24-5-million

[17] https://en.wikipedia.org/wiki/List_of_largest_sports_contracts

[18] John Majors, *True Identity* (Bethany House Publishers, 2017), 14.

[19] http://persocite.francite.com/blaisepascal/page9.html

[20] https://www.theexcellencecentre.org/tec/wisdom/

[21] https://www.biblestudytools.com/bible-study/topical-studies/15-amazing-attributes-of-god-what-they-mean-and-why-they-matter.html

[22] https://guideposts.org/inspiring-stories/stories-of-faith-and-hope/meeting-mother-teresa-led-him-to-a-life-of-service/

[23] https://www1.cbn.com/cbnnews/entertainment/2018/january/tim-tebow-rsquo-s-nbsp-shocking-story-about-john-3-16-lsquo-coincidence-rsquo-goes-viral

[24] Benjamin Breckinridge Warfield. In his sermon "God's Immeasurable Love," https://www.ligonier.org/learn/articles/what-does-world-mean-john-316

[25] https://www.biblestudytools.com/bible-study/topical-studies/what-are-the-four-types-of-loves.html

[26] http://billjohnsononline.com/the-great-blondin/

[27] https://news.gallup.com/poll/393737/belief-god-dips-new-low.aspx

[28] David Jeremiah, *God Loves You* (Faith Words, New York, 2012), 135.

[29] According to the U.S. Census Bureau, 18.4 million children, 1 in 4, live without a biological, step, or adoptive father in the home.

[30] https://www.baptistpress.com/resource-library/news/as-titanic-sank-he-pleaded-believe-in-the-lord-jesus/

[31] https://www.cdc.gov/nchs/fastats/health-expenditures.htm

[32] https://yeshuahboyton.com/42-miracles-of-jesus-in-order/

[33] https://yeshuahboyton.com/all-29-miracles-in-the-book-of-acts-in-chronological-order/

[34] Craig S. Keener (1960) is a North American academic, Charismatic Baptist pastor, theologian, Biblical scholar and professor of New Testament at Asbury Theological Seminary.

[35] https://www.christianitytoday.com/ct/2014/november/god-always-heals.html

[36] https://www.webmd.com/a-to-z-guides/news/20210325/gen-x-millennials-in-worse-health-than-prior-generations

[37] https://www.jesusfilm.org/blog/all-the-healings/

[38] Randy Alcorn, *Happiness* (Tyndale House, Carol Stream, IL. 2015), 377.

[39] https://thecove.org/blog/attributes-of-god-goodness/ (Christine Batchelder)

[40] https://www.zocalopublicsquare.org/2020/02/06/how-the-1913-gettysburg-reunion-came-to-be-the-greatest-gathering-of-conqueror-and-conquered-in-history/ideas/essay/

[41] https://relevantmagazine.com/faith/11-brother-lawrence-quotes-will-challenge-how-you-practice-faith/

[42] https://churchleaders.com/pastors/free-resources-pastors/145403-brother-lawrence-free-ebook-the-practice-of-the-presence-of-god.html

[43] Ibid.

[44] https://www.crosswalk.com/faith/spiritual-life/how-god-is-like-a-wild-goose.html

[45] https://www.gotquestions.org/God-omnipresent.html

[46] https://www.baslibrary.org/biblical-archaeology-review/42/3/2

[47] https://www.blueletterbible.org/lexicon/g2427/esv/mgnt/0-1/

[48] https://www.psychologytoday.com/us/basics/anxiety

[49] Don Everts, *Jesus With Dirty Feet* (Downers Grove, IL.: InterVarsity, 1999), 26-27.

[50] Compiled by F.E. Marsh

[51] https://www.blueletterbible.org/lexicon/g461/esv/mgnt/0-1/

[52] https://zondervanacademic.com/blog/the-seven-churches-of-revelation-why-they-matter-and-what-we-can-learn

[53] https://www.census.gov/data/tables/time-series/demo/income-poverty/historical-income-households.html

[54] https://www.brookings.edu/blog/up-front/2019/06/25/six-facts-about-wealth-in-the-united-states/

[55] https://blogs.bcm.edu/2021/09/22/whats-behind-the-increase-in-plastic-and-cosmetic-surgery/

[56] https://www.brainyquote.com/quotes/felicity_jones_786263

[57] https://www.forbes.com/billionaires/

[58]https://www.patheos.com/blogs/carlgregg/2012/03/lectionary-commentary-john-316-the-rest-of-the-story-for-sunday-march-18-2012/
[59]https://outreachmagazine.com/interviews/64015-timothy-keller-becoming-stewards-of-hope-part-1.html

Made in USA - North Chelmsford, MA
1379774_9798397686723
08.18.2023 1233